Third Place Learning

Reflective Inquiry Into Intercultural and Global Cage Painting

A volume in
Teaching<~>Learning Indigenous, Intercultural Worldviews:
International Perspectives on Social Justice and Human Rights

Series Editor:
Tonya Huber-Warring, *St. Cloud State University, Minnesota*

Teaching<~>Learning Indigenous, Intercultural Worldviews: International Perspectives on Social Justice and Human Rights

Tonya Huber-Warring, Series Editor

Growing a Soul for Social Change:
Building the Knowledge Base for Social Justice (2008)
edited by Tonya Huber-Warring

Third Place Learning

Reflective Inquiry Into
Intercultural and Global Cage Painting

by

Glyn M. Rimmington and Mara Alagic
Wichita State University

Information Age Publishing, Inc.
Charlotte, North Carolina • www.infoagepub.com

Library of Congress Cataloging-in-Publication Data

Rimmington, Glyn M.
 Third place learning : reflective inquiry into intercultural and global cage painting / by Glyn M. Rimmington and Mara Alagic.
     p. cm. -- (Teaching Learning Indigenous, Intercultural Worldviews: International Perspectives on Social Justice and Human Rights)
 Includes bibliographical references and index.
 ISBN 978-1-59311-926-3 (pbk.) -- ISBN 978-1-59311-927-0 (hardcover) 1. Intercultural communication--Web-based instruction. I. Alagic, Mara. II. Title.
 HM1211.R56 2008
 303.48'202854678--dc22

                                                                        2008020560

ISBN 13: 978-1-59311-926-3 (pbk.)
          978-1-59311-927-0 (hardcover)

Copyright © 2008 IAP–Information Age Publishing, Inc.

Printed in the United States of America

To our future:
Alexander and Anne Rimmington, Irena, Gorjan, Kellie, and Adrian Alagic

CONTENTS

ACKNOWLEDGMENTS

It was an honor for both of us to collaborate with many colleagues from academia, industry, and schools along with students, who participated in educational projects. These involved global learning, cage painting, and intercultural communication activities from which ideas for this book emerged. We would like to acknowledge the collaborative work of visionaries from the Boeing Company and Wichita State University that led to provision of resources to support the global learning program.

ABSTRACT

The hybridity and dynamism of today's interconnected, interdependent, and culturally diverse world pose challenges and opportunities for learning and communication. This book introduces an approach to facilitate global learning opportunities, while facing these challenges. The approach is based on the *cage painting* metaphor for dialogic coconstruction of meaning, and understanding of multiple perspectives. Resolving disorienting dilemmas or preconceptions requires a dialectic flow of thinking since the root of the problem may be situated deep within a person's beliefs and values. Such experiences might be transformative in their nature, involving: a change in person's perspective; better understanding the culture of themselves and other people; reflection and mindful inquiry into one's worldview;—third place learning. Misunderstandings are more prevalent when using technology—global reach— between people from distant locations or different cultures. To prepare people for these challenges, we offer a Web 2.0-based instructional design blueprint. Depending on the context and content of the planned activities, the cage painting and global learning processes may be facilitated simultaneously or sequentially. The approach to improving intercultural/global communication and collaboration presented in this book has attracted the interest of educators in different disciplines as well as human resource leaders. This approach emerged from 6 years of studying ways in which we, and our colleagues from 25 other countries, integrated global learning into classrooms in a range of discipline areas. In this book we explore the competences needed to communicate interculturally and to avoid the effects of preconceptions on our communication and collaboration. We review metaphors commonly used in intercultural communication and then introduce a new metaphor called *cage painting*. The process of cage painting requires certain conditions during intercultural communication, both for face-to-face or when using global reach, via technology.

FOREWORD

J. Michael Adams and Angelo Carfagna

The extraordinary philosopher and inventor Buckminster Fuller marked the date of August 6, 1945, as "the day that humanity started taking its final exam." The test continues today and like many exams, the questions seem to grow harder by the minute. The terrifying power of the atomic bomb dropped on Hiroshima has been dwarfed by much more lethal instruments of destruction. As conventional and unconventional weapons proliferate, the dangers escalate, but deadly violence is just one part of a worrisome equation.

Globalization, propelled by rapid technological advances, has connected cultures and countries, and linked human destinies. Of course, there are many benefits to globalization. Dollars, euros, and yens, as well as goods, products, ideas, and information flow today effortlessly across borders. They have produced for millions rising living standards, better government and services, improved education and medical care, and enriching cultural experiences. At the same time, though, globalization is fraught with troubles. Many blame it for spreading economic inequalities, pandemic diseases, environmental dangers and cultural conflicts, as well as terror and violence.

Globalization has greatly complicated humanity's final exam because it promises such wonders but threatens such misery. The pressure to get the answers right has never been greater. And the speed of globalization has thus far outraced our ability to comprehend the changes and understand the diverse peoples and cultures that are now bound so tightly to a common fate.

Education must help us catch up. And quickly. It will not be easy, though. We have had centuries to learn how to think locally and then nationally. We have long been taught to first and foremost take pride in and protect our "own." As philosopher Kwame Anthony Appiah has written in his book *Cosmopolitanism: Ethics in a World of Strangers*, the challenge "is to take minds and hearts formed over the long millennia of living in local troops and equip them with ideas and institutions that will allow us to live together as the global tribe we have become" (Apiah, 2006, p. xiii).

The resistance to global learning is enormous. After all, as Appiah has further observed, if you think or have been conditioned to believe you live on a city on a hill, you will not like the educational system pointing out that you are just one part of the whole. The quicker we learn that lesson, though, the better we will do on our final exam. We are one part of the whole. And we need to learn how to work and collaborate with other parts to combat the challenges of globalization. Our interests are the same.

If humanity is to pass its final exam, we will need more study guides like the one that Glyn Rimmington and Mara Alagic have provided. With the clever and compelling metaphor of cage painting, the authors have offered us a place (The Third Place) where global learning processes can flourish. The authors have provided strong educational strategies that teachers and faculty can use to help students enhance their intercultural communications skills and improve their understanding of other cultures.

The book is based on 6 years of global learning projects across disciplines that have involved students from around the world. It draws on theoretical and applied literature in the areas of education, intercultural communication, philosophy, psychology, and cultural studies. It takes us beyond the standard approaches that all too frequently are based on stereotypes of "national" cultures but do not help individual interactions. By focusing on intercultural communication competence, Rimmington and Alagic get to the heart of global interactions.

We would do well to heed their strategies. We would do well to focus more heavily on introducing global lessons and perspectives into our schools. Globalization must be answered with global education. And global education is perhaps best achieved through informed and meaningful global conversations.

So, with pencils pressed tightly against the page, we continue taking our final exam. We again think back to the dawn of the atomic age. Einstein was once asked what was the scientific antidote to the bomb. He replied, "There is no scientific antidote; the only antidote is education." Today's global challenges demand that we empower and educate students to think and act globally. It's the only way for humanity to pass the test.

PREFACE

What was the latest miscommunication or disorienting dilemma in your life?

Rimmington and Alagic

An anonymous reviewer of our manuscript wrote, the name Simea, "may cost the authors['] and editor['s] credibility." What a disorienting dilemma for us! How and why did this happen?

In a quest to create the practical implementation of a new conceptual framework for understanding intercultural communication, we worked with a number of collaborators to develop a simulator. The intent was for the learner to interact with a synthetic character from an unknown cultural background in order to clarify a miscommunication. The first name that we used for the synthetic character was *Sim*. Not everyone liked it. We did some research and tried various sim-names: Simon, Simone, Simantha, Simmo.... Finally, we settled on *Simea*. The name Simea appeared culturally neutral as much as we were able to conceptualize at the time. The main rationale was to avoid the learner lapsing into the use of stereotypes for a particular cultural group. Simea's character has a high level of intercultural communication competence. Simea would simultaneously be a mentor, coach, model and interactant from an unknown culture. As the simulation proceeds, Simea guides the learner in resolving a hypothetical miscommunication and understanding Simea's perspective in the given context. Simea is a good, helpful, patient character, who will help the learner to improve his/her intercultural communication strategies.

The reviewer was informing us about a particular interpretation of a variant of this name and encouraging us to clarify how we decided to use the name Simea. When we were choosing the name Simea with her place of origin being Simealand, we used *Simean* to express her unknown culture.

Unbeknown to us at the time, this became the source of a disorienting dilemma, since Simean is a homophone for the word *simian*. According to Merriam-Webster Online Dictionary, this word means: "of or pertaining to an ape or monkey." It was not our intention to have a learner to do cage painting with a monkey! We hope this book gets published! It is too late for us to redesign all the simulations, Web 2.0 learning objects and disown all earlier publications about the cage painting simulator. We encourage the reader to use our originally intended meaning of Simea as well as to realize the significance of carefully contextualizing intercultural interactions and the dangers of stereotyping.

Mara Alagic and Glyn Rimmington
—March 2008

INTRODUCTION

This introduction consists of two sections: Our Stories and Book Overview. *Our Stories* section captures our motivation, way of communicating and thinking about our own inquiry into intercultures and Third Place Learning in today's world. The second section, *Book Overview*, describes briefly how the book is conceptualized, including the need, background, and potential readers and different ways in which the book can be read and used in education and professional development.

OUR STORIES

First Story: Overcoming Cultural Preconceptions

In the process of developing our cage painting approach we often went back to discuss Glyn's conversation during an international visit about a cultural preconception that we named *Smiles*. Although it might appear as a simple preconception for some, customs that we are not used to might significantly affect our behavior. We used this experience to design a simulation from which others can learn about resolving cultural misconceptions and acquiring intercultural communication strategies. This opened the doors for considering many other misconceptions and developing more general strategies that might help in challenging intercultural situations. The following is a very short excerpt from that conversation with follow up reflection and contextualization.

People in the hotel here do not smile, unless they know you well. It is not a habit. But you will find them efficient.

I was puzzled and looked at my host, Simea, quizzically.

Glyn, they are not being rude. They just don't smile as much as you are used to.

Glyn felt somewhat disoriented by what to him was unusual behavior—people not smiling. He had been thinking of various explanations. Could it be that because this was a domestic hotel, not one for international guests, the staff and guests did not like foreigners? Simea quickly dispelled this and other explanations, but he remained puzzled since never in his travels had he encountered hotel staff or fellow guests, who did not offer a smile and friendly greeting. In his experience a hotel receptionist always greets new guests with a warm smile and welcoming words. He could not tell whether they were offering friendly greetings, since his command of the local language was limited. Obviously, he needed to rethink smiling as a custom. His understanding of smiles was ingrained so, it was not simple to both not smile and accept that others will not smile in return even if he smiles.

Glyn's Journal Entry

This was my first time in this country. My host, Simea, who had visited my country, met me at the airport and arranged for us to be driven to my hotel for this visit. On the way in, I practiced some simple phrases in the local language and my pronunciation seemed to work for the few words that I had learned. Simea explained that the hotel for international guests was closed for renovations and therefore I would be staying at a domestic hotel on the city square. She helped me to check in and negotiate my way to my room and we agreed that I would rest until it was time for an evening meal. In the course of going to my room and later returning to the lobby, I interacted with a number of staff. The receptionist in the lobby inspected my passport and had me fill in various forms, before allocating a room by handing me a piece of paper, but no key. We then took the lift to the 5th floor. We were met by a lady, who asked for the piece of paper from the reception. This piece of paper was exchanged for a room key. Apparently, I should swap the key for the piece of paper later and keep it so I would be permitted entry into the hotel. None of this surprised me. I had encountered such arrangements before in my travels to other places. What bothered me was that nobody smiled.

None of the staff returned a smile at any time. As I attempted to smile at some of them, it appeared to me that they looked at me in a quizzical fashion. As I reflected on this, I thought of various explanations. It could be that I was a foreigner in a domestic hotel and that they did not like foreigners?

Maybe the staff did not like their jobs? Perhaps the cold weather with ice, snow, bitterly cold wind and overcast sky outside made them depressed? Could it be that they were not paid very well, so they only did these jobs to get by? As I greeted other guests, who were locals, judging by their attire, they did not return a smile either. They did not smile to each other. Travel for them in this part of the world might not have been a happy experience. Again, it may be that they did not like or trust foreigners. All sorts of thoughts were running through my mind. So when Simea came to pick me up, I would ask her what this was about. I was even contemplating that I should complain about this hotel and ask to stay somewhere else. That could be seen as being an ungracious guest, but it did seem an unfriendly place.

I returned to the hotel lobby at the agreed time to be picked up by Simea. Once I was in the car with her, I asked, "Simea, why are the hotel staff so unfriendly?" She looked puzzled and asked, "Glyn, why do you think they are not friendly?" "The staff never smile," I explained. She asked, "Have they been efficient in providing service?" I could not fault them on the quality of their service. "The service has been fine," I replied. Simea explained, "In this *place*, Glyn, people do not smile when meeting others unless they have known each other for a long time." I told her, "I find this very strange, since *where I am from*, people almost always greet each other with a smile to show that they are happy and to help the person they are meeting feel happy." For me this was a substantial change to my outlook on smiling. "Simea, you know from your visit to my part of the world that everyone smiles when they meet other people. The receptionist in the hotel, where you stayed, smiled and offered a friendly greeting," I shared. She nodded. "If you were me and your experience had always been that people smile a lot and you were coming to this place, how would you adapt?" I was trying to get Simea to think of things from my perspective. "Glyn, you should not feel concerned by the lack of smiling. People here show their friendliness in other ways. The hotel staff will be efficient and courteous, but it is not their habit to smile. You can keep smiling but try to feel okay, when they do not return a smile. It will be okay."

Any true understanding is dialogic in nature.

Voloshinov (1929/1973, p. 102)

Glyn's Journal Entry 2

Later in the week, when I conducted a workshop on cage painting as a technique for improving intercultural communication, I was able to share this experience. Simea's students at the Center for Intercultural Communication found it interesting how Simea and I used a dialog to coconstruct new meaning for smiles and that we were able to negotiate an acceptable resolution. Simea had the advantage of having already been to where I am from, so she could be an intercultural mentor as I was trying to understand her cultural custom and fit it into my way of thinking about people's smiling habits.

Glyn's Journal Entry 3

I wonder what other cultural dilemmas I will face during my visit. To improve as an interculturalist, I need more practice at painting cages and intercultural learning. I also pondered about cultural preconceptions that might trigger cultural incidents when people of very distinct cultures are communicating via technology.

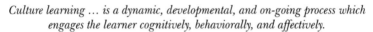

> Culture learning ... is a dynamic, developmental, and on-going process which engages the learner cognitively, behaviorally, and affectively.

Paige, Jorstad, Paulson, Klein, and Colby (1999, p. 50)

Let's speculate and generalize for a moment; consider the antithesis in this dialectic. Suppose Glyn refused to accept the practice of people not smiling and had been hostile to Simea, maintaining an ethnocentric stance, based on the view that his culture was superior to Simea's and people should just smile to accommodate him. He would hold this position thinking that these people are ignorant about the cultures of the rest of the world. Generalizing, from such a stance, Glyn would maintain that Simea and her students should be grateful that he had come to give them his *superior* knowledge.

The combination of continual migration and international travel has resulted in hybridization of cultures. The world is a complex place even for the experienced traveler or international collaborator. Generalizing and stereotyping are hidden dangers of intercultural interactions. A guidebook to the characteristics of each national culture is no longer of much value as you discover regional variation and the effects of hybridity. For example, when you visit some collaborators in India, you may discover that the person with whom you are interacting has parents from different provinces—maybe Kerala and Punjab—or even different countries—India and Singapore—possibly of different religions—Hindu and Buddhist. The person could have been educated in Australia, where they learned to speak Russian and then have traveled extensively in Russia. Their professor in Australia, who was born in China, but who had been educated in the United States and then married someone from the Philippines, might have been quite influential for him or her. What is an alternative to the national culture guidebook that can help to effectively resolve cultural misunderstandings and miscommunication? This alternative needs to be relatively easy to learn and should be effective in all situations. Not only should it have utility during face-to-face meetings, it also needs to be helpful for online interactions, using modern communication technologies. When using technology, we do not always have the benefit of nonverbal signals or the subtleties of intonation that can make interactions with our collaborators more mindful.

In this book we explore the competences needed to communicate interculturally and avoid the effects of preconceptions on our communication and collaboration. We review metaphors commonly used in intercultural communication and then discuss a metaphor called *cage painting*. The process of cage painting requires certain conditions during intercultural communication, whether it is face-to-face or via global reach, using technology. The transformative processes that we undergo as we confront culturally disorienting dilemmas, smiling being a simple example of one, are named the *Third Place Processes*.

Second Story: Global Reach and Third Place Processes

Exciting and challenging collaborative work can be carried out using communication technology tools. This is a place to mention many of our conversations, between the two authors and among the authors and their international colleagues across the world. The following section is a combination of excerpts adapted from these Internet-based chats and our reflections, through quotes, about the processes studied and developed in this book.

[9:53:44 PM] Simea says: *Good morning!* [Thursday night; Simea is in Simtown]

[9:55:26 PM] Learner says: *Good evening Simea* ☺ [Friday morning in Simville]

[9:56:02 PM] Learner says: *What challenge do you have for me tonight?*

[9:57:15 PM] Learner says: *I had a very busy day and did not have much time to ponder our conversation from last night.*

[9:58:41 PM] Simea says: *Let's play around with the idea of contexts; I find this fascinating.*

[10:00:01 PM] Learner says: *Well, what about cage painting scenarios from the point of view of contexts and contents?*

[10:00:47 PM] Simea says: *We are formulating global learning in terms of different contexts (two or more individuals communicating) and contextual distances.*

[10:01:17 PM] Learner says: *What do you mean by contextual distances?*

[10:02:31 PM] Simea says: *For every participant using global reach you have to consider both their context (cultural, professional) and their meaning structure (very connected to context) ...*

[10:02:44 PM] Learner says: *Contextual distance …*

[10:03:17 PM] Learner says: *I am immersed here in my context, you in yours.*

[10:04:25 PM] Simea says: *We only communicate in the evening (my time) and your morning. So it is very different than you being here as an Simlandic or me being in Simland as an Simean.*

[10:06:06 PM] Learner says: *Oh, contextual distance is different if I am in Simville and we meet for lunch—I am more aware of your context, your circumstances and even in what some elements of your meaning structure might be (than being here …)*

[10:06:15 PM] Simea says: *This is making sense, isn't it?* ☺

[10:06:28 PM] Learner says: *Yes.* ☺

[10:07:08 PM] Learner says: *Are there only two different contexts? Or are there also various other contexts that are in states of transition such as the one where we interact?*

[10:07:49 PM] Simea says: *Oh, it is more complex; it is just easier to illustrate it like this.*

[10:08:36 PM] Simea says: *You could say that the one in which we are communicating has certain characteristics of hybridity…*

…

To understand another person's utterance means to orient oneself with respect to it, to find the proper place for it in the corresponding context. For each word of the utterance that we are in the process of understanding, we, as it were, lay down a set of our own answering words. The greater their number and weight, the deeper and more substantial our understanding will be.

Voloshinov (1929/1973, p. 102)

…

[10:09:31 PM] Learner says: *Where are you up to on the book?*

[10:09:31 PM] Simea says: *Just revising chapter 1.*

[10:10:17 PM] Learner says: *What is the first chapter of your book about?*

[10:10:54 PM] Simea says: *It introduces competences for intercultural communication that are needed to avoid the undesirable effects of misconceptions or disorienting dilemmas.*

[10:11:05 PM] Learner says: *How can we understand and develop such competences?*

[10:11:28 PM] Simea says: *Metaphors are useful for this purpose and in fact we introduce a new metaphor.*

[10:11:55 PM] Learner says: *I am familiar with the iceberg and rhizome metaphors for understanding culture, but what is this new metaphor?*

[10:13:50 PM] Simea says: *It is called the "cage painting" metaphor.*

[10:14:14 PM] Learner says: *Strange topic for a metaphor; it sounds very unusual. Does the first chapter explain it?*

[10:14:54 PM] Simea says: *It is not so unusual, since it is based on an existing metaphor that was developed by Hugh Mackay in Australia, the cage metaphor.*

[10:16:07 PM] Learner says: *What does one need to participate in cage painting?*

[10:16:19 PM] Simea says: *You need another person, with whom to have a dialog and you both need to be prepared for the dialectic thinking of the Third Place.*

[10:16:27 PM] Learner says: *Is the Third Place a new idea? I learned that dialectic was something developed by Marx that was related to communism and so could undermine democracy?*

...

Dialectic is the art of discourse by which we either refute or establish some propositions by means of question and answer on the part of the interlocutors.

Laertius (1925/2000, p. 319)

[10:17:25 PM] Simea says: *Where do you get these strange ideas? Marx lived and died before the Communist era. Dialectic is about a way of thinking and sometimes a way of conversing with others. The ancient Chinese and Indian cultures had dialectic thinking, although it was different to modern ideas about dialectic thinking.*

[10:20:58 PM] Learner says: *Where is the Third Place? Is it very big?*

[10:21:10 PM] Simea says: *The Third Place was described by Bhabha and has been written about by many authors. The Third Place is not really a place in physical sense; it is somewhat an abstract concept. It is not physical, unless you are getting mixed up with the Internet Café idea. Being in the Third Place is like stepping outside of your own culture and examining it and the culture of others from some other perspective. It is about processes through which you move beyond your current culture or interculture to a new interculture, a hybrid of your culture and that of the person you are interacting with ...*

It is that Third Space, though unrepresentable in itself, which constitutes the discursive conditions of enunciation that ensure that the meaning and symbols of culture have no primordial unity or fixity; that even the same signs can be appropriated, translated, rehistorisized and read anew.

Bhabha (1994, p. 55)

[10:21:33 PM] Learner says: *Hmm. Maybe I am in the Third Place now? I need to learn some more about the dialectic, too.*

[10:25:39 PM] Learner says: *The more I chat with you the more I realize that nothing stays the same. There are always new perspectives that I have never heard of.*

[10:26:02 PM] Simea says: *Yes. Change is a constant. It is the same for me. You are presenting me with a disorienting dilemma, when you say that in school you learned that dialectic thinking is a tool for communists to undermine democracy. I had never heard of such teachings. So I have to change my thinking at a deep level to appreciate the perspective of someone, such as yourself, who had learned something that to me is nonsensical.*

> *You must be the change you wish to see in the world.*
>
> —Mahatma Gandhi

BOOK OVERVIEW

The latent learning potential of the world population has been grossly underestimated as a result of prevailing mind-sets that limit the design of interventions to improve the evolution of the global learning environment.

Cavallo (2000)

The impetus for writing this book came from two directions. The first was awareness of cultural trends rooted in the twentieth century, which make communication and collaboration a challenge. The second is our experience trying to develop appropriate education strategies to prepare learners to meet these challenges.

The hybridity and dynamism of today's increasingly interconnected, interdependent and culturally diverse world poses challenges and opportunities for learning and communication. International and domestic migration has resulted in a world in which nations, regions or even cities are rapidly increasing in cultural diversity. Interaction among these culturally diverse individuals is resulting in hybrid intercultures. The interconnectedness of the world provided by modern communication technologies and air travel results in many external influences upon any one culture, causing it to change more rapidly than at any earlier time in human history. Cultural hybridity, diversity, and change are becoming commonplace features of modern society.

Our approach over the past 6 years has been to make use of the very technology that provides high levels of interconnectivity, or *global reach*, to provide learners with opportunities to collaborate globally as part of their education in a variety of discipline areas. The intent was to help them to improve their ability to communicate and collaborate with people of other cultures. However, implementing this approach was by no means straightforward. Among the many obstacles were differences in time zones and semester alignment, the overlay of differences in disciplinary cultures (engineering versus humanities versus fine arts versus business versus education), the limitations of technology-based communication, the unfamiliarity of faculty outside of education with appropriate learning strategies, and the anxiety of learners faced with radically different ways of learning. There were no readily available conceptual frameworks that we considered appropriate to meet these challenges. Such a conceptual framework was needed. The ideas presented in this book emerged from these 6 years of studying the ways in which we and our collaborators integrated global learning into classrooms in a number of different discipline areas, and in which learners were connected between more than 25 countries. We also learned a great deal from presenting our evolving framework to other educators around the world.

The conceptual framework and approach described in this book are based on the cage painting metaphor for dialogic coconstruction of meaning and adoption of multiple perspectives. Such learning often involves confronting and hopefully overcoming cultural preconceptions, disorienting dilemmas, cultural incidents or culture shocks. Resolution of these situations requires a dialectic flow of thinking since the root of the problem may lay very deep within a person's beliefs and values. Such resolutions might be transformative in their nature, causing a change in the person's perspective plus an improved understanding of their own culture and that of others. This does not necessarily mean that they change their core beliefs, but rather that they grow to appreciate or at least understand those of others. Experiences of this nature tend to encourage ongoing reflective and mindful inquiry into one's worldview, which is part of the *Third Place Processes*.

> *Learning intercultural communication would proceed better if it proceeded through relatively complex and carefully constructed simulations of culturally embedded institutional talk contexts, and focused not on rules but on strategies and critique.*

Young (1996, p. 182)

Windows of opportunity for the global interactions are small due to time zone differences and lack of semester alignment. Therefore we needed to adapt the conceptual framework so learners can prepare for such interactions. To this end, we developed a simulator based on the cage painting metaphor. This has evolved into a Web 2.0-based learning environment that can be used both for learning from simulations and to create new scenario-based simulations. Each simulation provides the learner with a different intercultural event. Practicing with the simulator ideally will result in the learning outcome of having developed an intercultural communication heuristic that can be applied during real interactions.

The theoretical framing for this book draws upon critical social theory, dialectic thinking, social constructivist learning, cognitive apprenticeship, reflective practice and analysis of transfer, metaphors and transformative learning. Its essential features of dialectic thinking, reflective inquiry, and possible transformation are captured in the notion of third place processes. All this is explored in sufficient detail that the reader can more readily appreciate the basis of cage painting and its application.

The 6 years during which the conceptual framework was developed also yielded insights into aspects of instructional design that incorporate global learning—intercultural communication using global reach—in such a way that it is a vehicle for achieving learning outcomes associated with particular discipline areas. This resulted in a context- and content-sensitive instructional design blueprint that accounts for internal catalysts and external factors. Internally, facilitation of such things as a socialization period, blending of cage painting with content or critical reflection is important, while externally it is necessary to be aware of the requirement for leadership support and the necessary infrastructure.

The approach presented in this book has attracted the interest of educators in different disciplines along with human resource leaders concerned with a key characteristic of today's global business workers, namely competence in intercultural/global communication and collaboration. Our book will be of interest to those, who wish to enhance their classes by incorporating global learning experiences or perhaps the development of improved intercultural communication to deal with local diversity. The latter provides challenges for the classrooms of inner urban schools or schools with a multicultural student population. Equally, human resource directors in global businesses or corporations will find the cage painting approach helpful to prepare staff for overseas assignments or for project teams with globally distributed members. Anyone, who wants to improve their ability to communicate or collaborate with others of different cultures can benefit from learning and practicing cage painting.

Our book is structured into four main chapters (Figure 1), which can be read in a different order depending on your interests. If you are not familiar with the cage painting metaphor, you should start with chapter 1. Even if you are familiar with cage painting, you may still find this chapter interesting, since we go into some depth about cultural metaphors. Also, we discuss the dialectic nature of cage painting and relate it to intercultural and global communication competences as well as to the cultural proficiency continuum. Chapter 1 introduces the third place processes and this is elaborated further in chapter 3. Chapter 2 follows on from chapter 1 by introducing the need for a tool with which to practice intercultural communication before or in parallel with real interactions. We described a learning environment that comprises a cage painting simulator and a

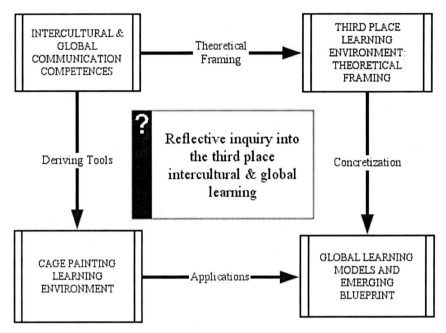

Figure 1.   Our essential question and concept map of relationships among four chapters.

repository of simulation scenarios to which more advanced learners can contribute. Chapter 2 expands on the cage painting concept by discussing an intercultural communication heuristic and its four constituent cage painting strategies. Simulation is compared with other ways of learning intercultural communication, such as role-plays and reading the intercultural literature. After a detailed treatment of the cage painting learning environment, we finish by describing nine laws of cage painting.

If you have an interest in where this conceptual framework fits within prevailing theoretical and philosophical bases, you will want to read chapter 3. If your interest is more on the practical side, you may wish to skip to chapter 4. However, if you wish to consider the theoretical framing of cage painting within critical social theory, dialectics, social constructivism, transformative learning and cognitive apprenticeship, then you will appreciate how these provide a ground for cage painting. Chapter 4 considers in more detail some of the global learning projects from the past 6 years that gave rise to the conceptual framework described in this book. It describes concrete applications from a variety of discipline areas and considers three in more detail as case studies. Something is learned from each venture irrespective of whether it was successful. This knowledge is consolidated into a

blueprint for instructional design that shows ways of facilitating opportunities for global and/or intercultural learning.

The chapters may be read from 1 through 4 for those, who are not
familiar at all with this approach. If you wish to first understand the experiential base from which the cage painting approach emerged, you should
read chapter 4 first. If you are more interested in the theoretical framing
of cage painting, chapter 3 is a must.

CHAPTER 1

INTERCULTURAL AND GLOBAL COMMUNICATION COMPETENCES

INTRODUCTION

In this chapter we consider a definition of culture within the framework of intercultural communication in both global and culturally diverse local settings. This leads to an examination of the *cage painting* metaphor, which represents dialogic coconstruction of meaning. Dialectic perspective is selected as a way of thinking about intercultural learning and communication. This perspective is helpful for developing an intercultural communication heuristic for resolving disorienting dilemmas that arise from cultural incidents. Overcoming such challenges requires a dialectic flow of thinking and cultural competence of interactants, both of which are introduced and elaborated upon in this chapter. In addition, we deliberate on intercultural and global communication competences and cultural proficiency continuum.

Third Place Learning: Reflective Inquiry Into Intercultural and Global Cage Painting
pp. 1–32

1

CULTURE

This section introduces the concept of culture via various cultural metaphors along with a dialectic view of cultural dimensions. These are precursors to our deliberations about intercultural communication competence in global and local, urban and rural contexts. Local contexts include the culturally diverse workplace or classroom. The latter is particularly important because of the disparity between the cultural backgrounds of teachers and that of their students, especially in urban schools. The global context is facilitated by the use of modern communication technologies: *global-reach*.

Within the context of intercultural communication, *culture* may be described as a shared system of knowledge about beliefs, values and norms that affect how people interact (Gudykunst, 1998; Ting-Toomey, 1999). A cultural community is usually perceived to share, "a sense of traditions, worldviews, values, rhythms, and patterns of life" (Ting-Toomey & Chung, 2005 p. 28). *Descriptive* definitions of culture attempt to list all aspects of activity encompassed by the word *culture* whereas *historical* and *genetic* definitions tend to emphasize heritage of tradition from past and present to future by considering the origin of the culture. The *normative* definition of culture represents shared rules for governance of the people's activity in a group, while the *psychological* definition of culture describes notions including habits, learning, adjustment and problem solution. Finally, a *structural* definition of culture describes organization or patterns of culture (Berry, Poortinga, Segall, & Dasen, 2002). Every aspect of people's lives is affected by their own culture, from individual to broader group functioning, the way of thinking, meaning making, expressing oneself, problem solving, organizing, and supporting a system of living (Hall, 1959, 1977).

Mary Jane Collier's (2005) operational definition of culture includes: "communicative location, a shared and contested alignment created by individuals, groups, organizations, or institutions; the location includes a history and itinerary and is both constrained by social structures and constructed through situated interaction" (p. 239). Within the changing landscapes of the global economies and communication media, our understanding of culture is that of being more of a dynamic than static entity, based on interactivity and ongoing dialog. As Wan Shum Eva Lam (2006) points out, conceptualization of culture is changing, "from stable identities, categorical memberships, and holistic traits to ways of *acting and participating* in diverse social groups and the heterogeneous sets of cultural knowledge, skills, and competence that are acquired in the process" (p. 217). Emerging from this view of culture is the need to integrate into our approach the critical and interpretative characteristics of dialectic thinking from Judith N. Martin and Thomas K. Nakayama's (1999) theorization of culture and communication.

CULTURAL METAPHORS

The Iceberg Metaphor of Culture

Consideration of cultural characteristics that allow people to know how to communicate with others from different cultures takes a prominent place in intercultural communication research (Gudykunst, 1998; Hall, 1977). The iceberg metaphor (Antal & Friedman, 2003) with its many layers underneath of water is a representation of culture as a visual tool used to convey both complexity and relative inaccessibility of many cultural characteristics within the context of intercultural communication. Layers are identified as surface level (popular culture), intermediate level (symbols, meanings, and norms), deep level (traditions, beliefs, and values), and underneath of it all, universal human needs (Ting-Toomey & Chung, 2005).

The *surface* level consists of representations that refer to obvious cultural artifacts and images that are acquired through a variety of media, from reading fiction to listening to a favorite daily news station, or from watching popular movies, to travel, and popular culture. We need to remember that these sources of information are often driven by economic motives (not educational motives), which involves crafting the information for very particular audiences. To avoid mindlessly stereotyping other cultures, in addition to being aware of images that we form based on superficial information, we need to critically evaluate the sources of information and their motives, while remaining "mindful that a culture exists on multiple levels of complexity" (Ting-Toomey & Chung, 2005, p. 31).

The *intermediate* level comprises symbols, meanings, and norms. Every culture has symbolic systems that inherently reflect shared meanings to members of that culture: a word, a phrase, a colloquial expression, or a nonverbal gesture. Subjective or objective interpretations that people of one culture attach to a certain symbol may be very different from the meaning that people of other cultures attach to the same symbol. This is similar to the different ways in which *yes* and *no* are symbolized or gestured in different cultures, and which can become a major obstacle for intercultural communication. According to Stella Ting-Toomey and Leeva C. Chung (2005) cultural norms encompass goals and expectations within a particular setting for participants of varying cultural competence.

The *deep* level is concerned with traditions, beliefs, and values that are shared by a group of individuals. Traditions include legends, holidays, various celebration ceremonies, and other customs that members of a cultural group share with a certain degree of appreciation and significance. Culturally shared beliefs can be defined as fundamental assumptions about human existence, concepts of space, time, and reality, and other closely related ideas or events. These beliefs are usually not questioned and meanings are given to phenomena based on these beliefs. Cultural values refer to the priority that a cultural group assigns to a desirable or nondesirable range of behaviors (Ting-Toomey & Chung, 2005).

Why Metaphors?

Metaphors and the related forms: similes and analogies; are three types of models that have been used to explain complex or difficult concepts since the earliest times. The metaphor has value in the educational context, but we need to understand its structure and limitations. The metaphor is a comparison and comprises two concepts and two relationships. There is the concept being explained, the *ground*, and the concept being used to explain the ground, the *topic*. Metaphors are usually named by their topic (e.g., *iceberg* metaphor of culture). The two relationships are first, the comparison between the ground and topic, the *vehicle* (intertextuality), and second, the *tension* arising from the dissimilarity between the topic and the ground (Figure 1.1). The latter is an inescapable characteristic of the dialectic nature of a metaphor (Gannon, 2001; Vaara, Tienari, & Säntti, 2003).

In the case of the iceberg metaphor, the ground is culture and the topic is the iceberg. Intertextuality is captured in the description of layers and the intent is to express the depth, complexity, and inaccessibility of some of the cultural characteristics. The question, *What do an iceberg and a culture have in common?* explicates the essence of potential tensions of this metaphor. The tension is even more explicit if we try to incorporate this metaphor into our thinking about intercultural interactions. Searching for a more appropriate cultural metaphor conducive to interactivity is one of the possible solutions.

Figure 1.1.   The iceberg metaphor: ground—culture, topic—iceberg, and two relationships—intertextuality and tension.

It is not just an implicit or explicit comparison that makes metaphors effective and powerful tools, but the construction of new meaning from interactions (translation) between the two different domains of meaning (ground and topic). George Lakoff and Mark Johnson (1980) in their interactionist view, argue that metaphors are omnipresent not only in language but also in social thoughts, actions and interactions. Furthermore, Lakoff and Johnson emphasized the significance of metaphors in constructing new meanings and understandings and thus the connection of cognition and action. The latter gives power to metaphors in a more encompassing way than a traditional rhetorical view would allow. Although the views of George Lakoff and Mark Johnson are criticized for overemphasizing the constitutive role of metaphors at the cost of neglecting other figures of speech, the fact remains that metaphors do give an insight beyond existing frameworks and convey meanings in concise ways (Vaara et al., 2003).

The three theses—*compactness, inexpressibility* and *vividness*—that explicate the properties of the metaphors (Gannon, 2001) are easily accounted for in the iceberg metaphor. The *compactness* thesis refers to the fact that the topic of a metaphor, as a mental picture of the ground, is in effect *worth a thousand words*. There are aspects of anyone's culture that are invisible to interactants even after a long period. The invisibility of the underwater part of an iceberg points to both, the compactness of the metaphor, and the fact that ground (culture) cannot be easily captured by words available to us; the *inexpressibility* thesis. This is also related to the dynamic nature of the flow of our experience that cannot be fully captured with discrete symbols, such as words. *Vividness* is about the implicit richness of representation (complexities of an iceberg) as we attempt to reconstruct a mental image of our experiences.

Good metaphors inspire both creative and critical thinking. They enable connection of emotional and perceptual experiences, as people attempt to share experiences with each other. As a result, metaphors tend to facilitate holistic mindfulness, which in turn can enhance intercultural communication. Therefore, in many ways, it is not only about what a metaphor is, it is what the metaphor does, for example, "tip the first domino" or "brain and mind as hardware and software."

As an educational tool, metaphors have both advantages and inherent limitations. Provided that the topic is something familiar in the learner's prior experiences, metaphor-based representations help with conceptual understanding and recall. Furthermore, the process (vehicle) of moving between the topic and ground is effective in developing deeper understanding of attributes/characteristics of the ground. Important limitations of a metaphor are any presuppositions that the listener may have about the topic. For a metaphor to be effective, the educator or learner needs to be aware of the listener's familiarity with the topic and perceptions of the topic.

Among the metaphors used to improve our understanding of culture, are the *French Wine* metaphor (Gannon, 2001), the *Software of the Mind* metaphor (Hofstede, 1991), the *iceberg* metaphor (Antal & Friedman, 2003), and the *Rhizome* metaphor (Clarke, 2000), the last of which we will now consider in more detail.

The Rhizome Metaphor of Cultural Identity

The cultural identity concept encompasses all the complexities of cultural characteristics as they relate to cultural attributes of an individual. The genealogical tree metaphor (Deleuze, Guattari, & Massumi, 1988) (Figure 1.2a) has been used to understand cultural identity. This metaphor captures many characteristics of cultural identity defined by ones' past lineage back to a common ancestor. However, part of the tension within genealogical tree metaphor may be illustrated by changes arising from intermarriages through generations and migration between the increasingly diverse societies of a globalized world. In a study of Antillaise (West-Indian) society Richard L. W. Clarke (2000, p. 12) quotes Richard Burton (1993, p. 16) "identity is no longer imagined as a single tree ... but as a tangled, proliferating growth, without beginning or end, containing within its myriad recesses infinite possibilities of interactive transformation." So, Richard Clarke puts forward a *rhizome* metaphor of cultural identity (Figure 1.2b).

The contrast between the two metaphors of cultural identity, the genealogical tree and rhizome, runs parallel with the contrast between an approach that assumes inherent positive outlook (Kim, 1994) and a systems approach (e.g., Bertalanffy, 1968; Boulding, 1985). Assigning positive values to cultural identity represents a dichotomous rather than a dialectic viewpoint. This dichotomous perspective does not reflect the reality that there is a negative side to any cultural identity; it may involve ethnocentric adoration of one's own culture while disrespecting that of others. Such ethnocentric behavior carried to its extreme, results in the exclusionist view of belonging to only one cultural identity, that into which a person was born. This may contribute to overemphasis of cultural homogeneity, which is at odds with the diversity of modern society. For example, Yun Young Kim (1994, p. 5) cites Maria Root (1993, p. 9) that in the United States, "a significant proportion of White-identified persons are of multiracial-multiethnic origins." This dichotomist and exclusionist perspective is not disputed to any great extent in cultural identity development theories. The implication is that development of cultural

Figure 1.2a.   A genealogical tree metaphor of
cultural identity.

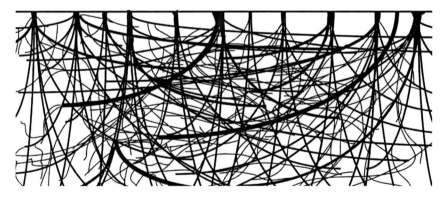

Figure 1.2b.   Tangled root mass of a rhizome, metaphor of cultural identity.

identity does not extend beyond enculturation during a person's formative
years, which is not consistent with the reality of new migrants' acculturation
within their host country (Kim, 1988, 1994) or dialogic coconstruction of
an evolving identity during global learning interactions (Alagic, Gibson, &
Rimmington, 2007).

Emerging from the above discussion is the need for a theoretical conceptualization of cultural identity, which encompasses the following:

(a) a person's cultural reach is not fixed (Hall, 1993);
(b) a change to identity does not mean eliminating a person's original identity;
(c) the boundaries of a person's cultural identity are permeable; and
(d) a person's identity allows for fluidity and openness toward differing cultural identities (United Nations Educational, Scientific and Cultural Organization, 2001).

A dynamic and evolving perspective of human existence views a person as an open system with the ability to learn and change in the course of and as a result of new experiences. This perspective allows for a succession of changes during which altered attitudes and behaviors are instilled into an individual's identity. It reflects a human potential to regulate the process of renewal while maintaining an overall stability (Kim, 1994).

A general systems approach (Bertalanffy, 1968; Boulding, 1985) captures the above characteristics of cultural identity. Instead of defining individual's cultural identity just in terms of its current state, Yun Young Kim (1994) posits the extension of the cultural identity construct to consider the question, "whom we may yet become[?]" (p. 9). She postulates that *intercultural identity* is a construct responding to that question and including a substantive component that allows, "emotional identification of oneself that is not limited to one's own social group but to other cultures as well" (p. 9). This point of view moves beyond a single group interest to one that allows for seeing and identifying with others' perspectives. It is essential to recognize that such identity perspective, which goes beyond basic cultural boundaries, is mediated relative to other cultures and therefore is closely related to intercultural interactions and communication activities. *An intercultural identity is not only about who thou is; it is also about who thou wants to be.*

BEYOND ICEBERGS AND RHIZOMES: THE CAGE METAPHOR

Both the iceberg and the rhizome metaphors serve to point out many complexities inherent in the concepts of culture and cultural identity. Analyzing these metaphors reveals the potential for dichotomous versus dialectic thinking about cultural characteristics, which in turn may impede the success of an intercultural interaction. Furthermore, these metaphoric expressions of cultures do not provide a clear insight into their implications for human interactions. In what follows we consider a cultural metaphor that will blend itself into a communication metaphor that is more appropriate for the purpose of this book.

In his book, *Why Don't People Listen? Solving the Communication Problem*, Hugh Mackay (1994) introduces the cage as a metaphor for the *effect of* life experience, cultural background, and current context upon an individual's view of the world. Such a cage is invisible, while the individual remains unaware of this effect. We specify the *invisible cage* concept as a metaphor for cultural identity, while considering cultural identity in the broadest sense to include all attributes that affect interactions with others; "the heterogeneous sets of cultural knowledge, skills, and competence that are acquired in the process [of interactions]" (Lam, 2006, p. 217). The cage affects the way in which individuals convey and interpret meaning for each other. The first rule of communication is *never blame the listener*. In other words it is incumbent upon the speaker to communicate in such a way that the listener will derive the intended meaning. Therefore he or she must understand his/her cage and that of the listener. This involves the speaker becoming more aware of his/her own cultural background, experiences, and context to improve the way he or she contributes to communication by learning more about the cultural background, experiences and context of the listener. The ultimate test of communication is whether the listener has understood the meaning as intended by the speaker. Like our cultural background or life experiences, the cage is inescapable.

The difference between the cage metaphor and the iceberg metaphor is that the cage corresponds to the subsurface part of the iceberg, which is not visible. The portion of the iceberg that is above the surface is what is seen without taking into account the individual's experience, background, or context—the superficial view. The cage represents both the intermediate and deep levels of the below-water portion of the iceberg: symbols, meanings, and norms, as well as traditions, beliefs, and values. The former is a symbolic system the individual uses to express a *point of view*. The latter reflects the *meaning structure*, or deeply held beliefs, values, norms, and traditions, of the individual. The meaning structure, for the most part, develops during enculturation into the individual's home culture. Diving below the surface to see deeper parts of the iceberg corresponds to conversing with the other person to discover some details of his/her cage; the longer and more probing the conversation, the better the cage can be *seen*. Early in the conversation, points of view are shared. After a longer time, the individuals may share deeply held beliefs. Sometimes this happens, when the individuals encounter a disorienting dilemma so intense that it goes beyond challenging their points of view, to challenge their meaning structure, and potentially prompt a revision of their meaning structures.

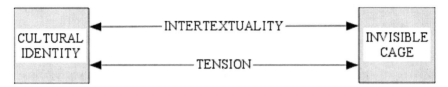

Figure 1.3.   Invisible cage metaphor relative to cultural identity: Intertextuality and tension relationships between the ground, cultural identity, and its topic, invisible cage.

Intertextuality, relative to invisible cage bars, refers to the challenge of negotiating the meaning of cultural characteristics, their depth, complexity, and inaccessibility. Incongruity between cultural characteristics and their metaphoric representations, the invisible bars, points to the other relationship between ground and topic of the cage metaphor, the tension (see Figure 1.3 above).

Every metaphor has its limitations, among which are: *vagueness, volatility,* and *imprecision*. But, if the context and intertextuality are given necessary consideration, it is possible to overcome these challenges and to utilize the intended characteristic of the metaphor under consideration (Vaara et al., 2003). During some presentations to different audiences some interpretations and negative reactions have been encountered about the cage. For instance, some people have felt that a *cage metaphor* is an oppressive idea akin to a prison, so they disliked it. However, its encapsulating quality is important for the metaphor to work since our perception of the world is an inescapable quality of our existence. Before seeing a diagram of the cage, some people imagined it to be a rectangular box with solid walls on three sides and bars on the front, as in the cage for a zoo animal or a jail. They imagined only the solid walls and thus significance of bars to reduce miscommunication was lost.

Cage Bars and Cultural Dimensions

How complex is someone's cage in terms of its bars and their arrangement? What do we need to know or find out about our cages for a successful interaction? One of the main challenges is to recognize their invisible complexity, without stereotypical presumptions. What is it that the invisibility is concealing? A complex hierarchy of overlapping cultural groupings from family to national or even global and including work, home, sports and others indicate that cage metaphor needs to be regarded as context sensitive. One way to elaborate on these challenges is to think about existing models of culture based on cultural dimensions, which can be captured by cage bars along with a multitude of other attributes.

Martin J. Gannon (2001) emphasized that reducing cultures to a set of dimensions has its limitations "describing cultural mind-sets used in daily activities, and ignore the institutional molding of these mindsets" (p. 236). In a similar manner, the cage is not limited to a particular set of bars. Keeping Gannon's observation in mind, it is still useful to consider some examples of dimensional models of culture. Dimensional language provides a certain vocabulary for characterizing cultural differences, as long as dimensions are not taken as ultimate: the only way of conceptualizing cultures.

Florence Rockwood Kluckhohn and Fred L. Strodtbeck (1961) proposed six dimensions to describe the assumptions of a society according to whether people are:

- Good or bad, or both
- Subjugate nature or live in harmony with nature?
- Oriented towards individualism or collectivism
- *Being* or *doing* society
- Perceiving public and private space differently
- Oriented towards the past, present, or future?

Edward Twitchell Hall (1966) focused on communication patterns along the four dimensions:

- Context and the level of explicit information required
- Space, especially personal space
- Time: monochromic versus polychromic orientation
- Information flow: the structure and speed of messages and communication.

Geert Hofstede (1991) developed a dimensional approach for describing national cultures in international business:

- *Power distance*: the disparity of power distribution in the society;
- *Uncertainty avoidance*: the degree of acceptance of uncertainty;
- *Individualism-collectivism*: the degree of self-versus group-orientation;
- *Masculinity-femininity*: the orientation towards aggressiveness;

- *Time orientation*: static tradition-oriented versus dynamic future-oriented.

According to Brent McSweeney (2002) the methods used to derive Geert Hofstede's (1991) dimensions lack research methodological validity. Someone could still argue that, theoretically, they do provide one way of looking at cultures. However, the theoretical lens based on Geert Hofstede's dimensions, or other similar approaches assumes that a single nation has a single culture, which can mislead a person when interacting with people from another country based on dimensional assumptions. Furthermore, formal conceptualization of *dimensions* in general assumes that they are independent, which is not the case in this model. An obvious illustration is the confounding relationship between Power distance and Gender dimensions (McCoy, 2003).

An application of lens metaphor based on a limited number of dimensions has some additional inherent risks, such as: *cultural agnosia*, lack of *cultural acuity*, and the *Heisenberg uncertainty* effect (Rimmington, Gibson, & Alagic, 2007). Cultural agnosia, the first risk, refers to the fact that the designers' cultural background affects their conceptualization of dimensions. Suppose the designer is from a culture in which alcohol consumption is acceptable and so the designer assumes that is a characteristic of any culture. The lens is therefore deficient, when it comes to characterizing the national culture of the Kingdom of Saudi Arabia, where alcohol is banned. Generalizing further, cultural habits related to food are not captured by the above dimensions, although these are very relevant during intercultural interactions. Having only five dimensions with which to depict a culture leads to a lack of cultural acuity, the second risk. For example, time may be a dimension of national culture (Tuleja, 2005). However, it can be divided into many subsidiary meanings. Some may be more important than others, depending on the context. Priorities between family and work time, punctuality, need for planning or use of windows of times rather than specific times, are a few examples. The third risk, the Heisenberg uncertainty effect, is perhaps the most significant. The lens itself affects the perception of culture. The designer's culture affects the *shape* of the lens through which other cultures are viewed. In ethnographic and anthropological fieldwork, Margaret Mead (1928) advocated the need to pay attention to this to remove or at least take into account the effects of the observer on the observations. Tabular guides to the cultures of other countries, based on the lens metaphor, usually present distorted impressions of the other cultures and an overly complimentary representation of the culture of the author (e.g., Hodge, 2000, pp. 71-75, Table 4.1).

In the authors' experiences of interacting with people from other cultures, two things are apparent: diversity and dynamics. First, for example, in China, there are 56 distinct ethnic groups each with their own linguistic and cultural characteristics (Sun, 1989). Further, in China the *culture* changes depending on whether an interaction is *official*, that is, involving Chinese Communist Party members or *unofficial* involving nonmembers. Globally, because of immigration, it is possible to meet a person of almost any ethnic background living in any given country. Such a person may exhibit characteristics of their original ethnicity blended with that of the host country in proportions that will vary on an individual basis. We therefore argue that the quest for a *lens* based on a limited set of dimensions, as described above, does not provide for refinement of intercultural understanding through interaction between the people from different cultures. It is akin to trying to use a national climatic averages map to forecast tomorrow's weather for a given town within the country. An approach is needed that provides for revision of meaning, finer resolution and dialogic interpretation; an approach based on an interactive process rather than on ethnocentric interpretations. In this sense the number and arrangement of bars in the cage metaphor is unlimited, thus reflecting the complexity of culture at the level of individual interactions.

All of the above-mentioned approaches provide significant insight into an understanding of broad national culture similarities and differences. In turn, these need to be complemented with additional consideration to the various cultural groups and subgroups to which an individual belongs, membership of which are reflected in the behavior of that individual. For example an individual lives in a particular state, city, neighborhood, family, has a certain ethnicity, gender, age, educational level, profession, religion, works for a certain company, plays certain sports, has hobbies and so on. Each of these contributes to the individual's bricolage of cultural characteristics and affects their intercultural communication. Understanding this requires a different approach to that used at the national level. Our conclusion is that a dialectic approach is called for.

Judith N. Martin and Thomas K. Nakayama (1999) view culture from an intercultural communication point of view and propose a dialectic approach to dimensions. The approach they propose is somewhat open-ended; there are always more dialectics to be considered. For those dimensions of culture with a dialectic nature, cage bars capture one's position on a dialectic continuum. Characterizing culture at the level of an individual is not just a matter of the number of dialectics to consider, but also change within the dialectics (Gudykunst, 2005). Culture cannot be assumed to be static, because of the motion in relation to a network of interacting dialectics. Individuals belong to various groups and may have multiple roles within these groups, for example as a parent and spouse within a family and as a teacher, advisor and researcher within a university culture. As the individual moves between these roles, either physically or conceptually, their cultural bricolage adjusts—their cage changes.

INTERCULTURAL COMMUNICATION: DIALECTIC PERSPECTIVE

Integrating culture into communication theories is a typical way in which theoretical frameworks for intercultural communication are established. William B. Gudykunst (2005) identifies several such approaches: culture can be integrated with the communication processes in communication theories; theories can be designed to describe how communication varies across cultures; or theories can be generated in an attempt to explain communication between people from different cultures. Most of the theorists have considered intergroup communication, assuming that culture is just one of the factors influencing communication, and that the constituent intercultural communication processes are similar.

In this book we give a significant place to a dialectic thinking perspective of intercultural communication, based on Martin and Nakayama's (1999) dialectic approach to theorizing about culture and communication. Critical and interpretative characteristics of dialectic thinking appear to be essential for our deliberations on intercultural interactions. The dialectic approach to intercultural communication combines three traditional approaches, that of social science, the interpretative, and the critical.

Understanding and participating in any intercultural communication, requires careful consideration of the four components, *culture* and *communication* as fundamental, and *environment* and *power* as background or contextual but not less relevant components. The dialectic approach recognizes both the need and the significance of understanding multiple perspectives and the consequent, potentially contradictory nature of intercultural communication. Cultures change, as do individuals, which brings into focus the holistic rather than reductionist aspects of intercultural communication and questions the capability of people to hold contradictory ideas simultaneously. This notion may be difficult to comprehend because it challenges educational approaches that rely on dichotomy and single answer thinking; "a dialectical approach requires that we transcend dichotomous thinking in studying and practicing intercultural communication" (Martin & Nakayama, 1999, p. 63)

Acknowledging different perspectives on a particular issue may be viewed as photographing a given object from different angles. No single angle provides all the information, but taking several photos, each from a different angle, allows formation of a more comprehensive understanding of the object. However, when people are the topic in question, different perspectives might be based on tightly held cultural beliefs and values, making it very difficult to accept others' perspectives as valid and useful. Martin and Nakayama (1999) formulate some of the intercultural communication dialectics that can serve as a basic framework for conversations among interacting individuals from both very similar and very different cultures.

Cultural-Individual

The norms and behaviors of the group and individual's behavioral traits are dynamically related and sometimes at odds or in a state of tension. Although it appears that we can deduce the behavior of an individual member from general cultural characteristics, or infer from the individual's behavior something about the cultural group characteristics, this is not the case. That interesting interplay of cultural and individual can be illustrated with the following example. An American, who is a migrant from Bosnia, will display certain behaviors, such as preparing Bosnian food. This behavior cannot be inferred from American cultural norms, nor, can it be used to infer what American culture is. However, this person is still an *American*. For some, the conception of being an American is fixed and for others it is continually evolving.

Personal-Contextual

Changing behavioral characteristics depend on the context: mother to her children; teacher to her students; peer to her colleagues in her school; peer to her colleague in another country. An individual adjusts in a required context according to her/his own individual characteristics.

Differences-Similarities

Emphasizing only differences can lead to stereotyping; emphasizing only similarities can lead us to ignore important cultural variations. Both can lead to miscommunications. It is not possible to characterize an individual with just one (e.g., gender) or even a narrow set of attributes as we have observed above in the discussion of dimension models of culture. British, Australian, United States, and Canadian citizens for the most part speak English as a first language, however each of these countries has a different history, geography, system of government, and laws. So while, they may share a common language, that does not mean that citizens from each of these countries will have a similar culture; far from it. Modes of greeting between French, Americans, and Japanese citizens may be characterized as different; kissing both cheeks, shaking hands, and bowing, but it cannot be inferred that they always observe the same modes of greetings with fellow citizens of different status, gender, or age. Stereotypes of this kind could result in misunderstandings if applied without taking into account individual differences.

Static-Dynamic

Culture and communication may vary between being static or in flux, which in turn affects the relationship between them. Both static and dynamic aspects of culture and communication will affect intercultural interactions.

History/Past and Present/Future

There is a need to focus simultaneously on the past and the present to understand intercultural communication. For example the partition of Pakistan and India in 1947 affects the relationship between these countries and their citizens. The history of each cultural group plays an important role in the present nature of that group.

Privilege-Disadvantage

Each person or cultural group can have both privileges and disadvantages, depending on the context; sometimes the one trait can be simultaneously a privilege and a disadvantage.

How are you privileged and how are you disadvantaged while communicating with someone from a specific but distinct culture? For example, although as a migrant you might have a professional education that gives you an advantage in your new country, you could be disadvantaged in certain situations because of your foreign accent or incomplete fluency in the language of your new country. How will these characteristics affect your interactions? Consider other dialectics in a similar manner (Figure 1.4). Which of them might significantly affect your interactions?

We can think about the dialectic as being a lens through which we can view and analyze the complexities and dynamics of intercultural interactions. There are no simple answers in terms of synthesis from dilemmas, but rather we need to recognize multiple, contradictory viewpoints and be able to search for ways of successfully interacting in such circumstances. One needs to view processes and relationships in holistic terms. The above list is an initial set of dialectics that Martin and Nakayama (1999) offered

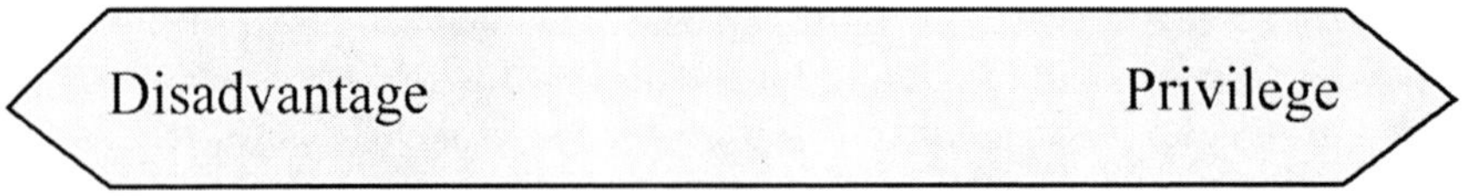

Figure 1.4.   Privilege and disadvantage during intercultural communication.

to initiate a somewhat structured entry into the dialectic way of thinking about cultures and intercultural communication. These examples of dialectics should facilitate understanding the perspectives of others. By allowing oneself to think along the continuum of various dialectics, consideration of multiple perspectives, sometimes contradictory to those strongly held by an individual, will receive appropriate consideration. This approach could help resolve disorienting dilemmas or critical incidents happening sometimes during intercultural interactions and develop shared points of view in a dialogic context.

THIRD PLACE: IN MEDIAS RES

The perspective of the stranger on the new culture is informed by experiences drawn from outside that system: stranger's native culture (Rogers, 1999). This quality brings new value to understanding the culture of one's own system and that of another place. Everett M. Rogers argues that if more attention had been paid to Georg Simmel's (1921) concept of the *stranger*, intercultural research would have focused more on the uncertainty involved in intercultural communication. Simmel's concept of the stranger bears similarities with the *marginal man*, a *cosmopolite*, and *citizen of the world* (Park, 1928). While the stranger may be viewed with suspicion or being *outside the system*, there are certain advantages to being a stranger, such as not being completely subject to the social norms of the system.

Imagine a situation in which two discussants can be *strangers* and thus can explore each other's cultural perspectives and his/her own with an open-mind toward both cultures. In modern days, when strangers interact through global reach, from their home locations, the idea of stranger has a different meaning and allows for this kind of interactions.

> It is that Third Space [place], though unrepresentable in itself, which constitutes the discursive conditions of enunciation that ensure that the meaning and symbols of culture have no primordial unity or fixity; that even the same signs can be appropriated, translated, rehistoricized and read anew. (Bhabha, 1994, p. 55)

Such processes have advantages for intercultural communication and the development of multiple perspectives because they allow for multiple voices to be heard, valued, interpreted and reinterpreted. The challenge is how to create the conditions that Bhabha (1994) describes. For example, awareness of and attention to the power relationship between teacher and student or interactants may encourage mutual trust (Bretag, 2006; Freire, 1968/1970). Further, time needs to be allowed at the beginning of an interaction for participants to learn more about each other and to become comfortable with claiming common ground and sharing social and personal information, all of which are catalysts for the third place processes. Similarly, the mode of communication needs to allow for time between interactions so that the interactants can reflect critically about each other's contributions. In other words, time needs to be allowed for the process of interpreting and considering alternatives (Ishii, 1984; Starosta & Chen, 2005). Deliberate pauses and active listening during communication are essential for achieving this process.

> Culture learning is the process of acquiring the culture-specific and culture-general knowledge, skills, and attitudes required for effective communication and interaction with individuals from other cultures. It is a dynamic, developmental, and on-going process which engages the learner cognitively, behaviorally, and affectively. (Paige, Jorstad, Paulson, Klein, & Colby, 1999, p. 50)

According to Anthony J. Liddicoat (2002) the process of cultural learning begins with knowledge of the practices of one's own culture and exposure to the practices of the new culture. Resulting practices may be (a) the same as in the original culture; (b) the same as in the new culture; or (c) a result of accommodating for both cultures, an original practice that is transformed or adjusted to fit the customs of the new culture. This synthesized system of cultural practices is called an *interculture* (Liddicoat, 2002). Liddicoat contends that one's original culture may itself be an interculture if one has parents from two different cultures.

As one is exposed to customs and practices of different cultures throughout one's life, one evolves through new intercultures. The intercultures may be regarded as steps within a continuing nonlinear process of cultural negotiation. This process involves a combination of retaining previous rules and practices, adapting some from the previous interculture and adopting some from the other culture. The process is shaped by the state of the four main variables: power relations, context, communication skills, and cultures. We refer to this continual synthesis of intercultures as the *third place processes*.

How is this *culture learning* related to our cage metaphor? What would be a way to metaphorically represent the process of culture learning and intercultural communication? In the following section we attempt to answer this question; we describe a metaphor and conceptual framework for visualizing and understanding this process of negotiating intercultural understanding as a third place process.

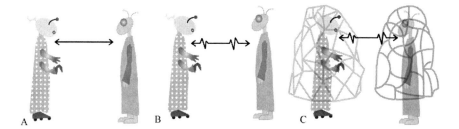

Figure 1.5. A: Idealized transfer of messages; B: Distortion of messages leading to misunderstandings; C: Invisible cages causing the distortion.

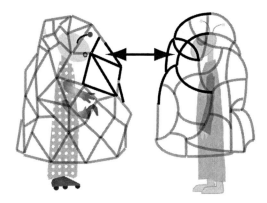

Figure 1.6. Cage painting allows for undistorted flow of communication.

CAGE PAINTING METAPHOR:
DIALOGIC COCONSTRUCTION OF MUTUAL UNDERSTANDINGS

An ideal portrayal of communication in which the participants always fully understand each other is shown in the Figure 1.5-A. The straight line represents the smooth *flow of the message* and implies that the recipient of a message interprets it exactly as the other person intended. Tacit content of the message is not obvious and may include cultural, contextual, nonverbal and other variables. Therefore, the reality is that something might interfere with our communication, resulting in misunderstandings (Figure 1.5-B). The squiggles in the line are used to represent the effects of these tacit variables. The squiggles can be accounted for by the exist-ence of each individual's invisible cage (Figure 1.5-C). The cage sur-rounds each individual and represents the effects of cultural background, life experiences and context on their perspective (Rimmington, Gibson, Gibson, & Alagic, 2004). It is conceptualized as initially being invisible, because it represents the inexplicable interference with communication that leads to misunderstandings, when one is not aware of one's own characteristics or those of other interactants.

Cage painting (Figure 1.6 above) refers to the process of developing a mutual understanding of one's own perspective and that of others. This is accomplished by becoming cognizant of the cultural backgrounds, life experiences of participants and the context of interactions during the dialog. It requires appropriate questioning techniques and willingness of participants to be responsive to each other's questions in a mindful manner. Successful cage painting reduces the chance of misconceptions and misunderstandings (Alagic, Gibson, & Rimmington, 2007; Rimmington, Gibson, & Alagic, 2007).

Cage painting is achieved through dialogic coconstruction of meaning and identity between people of different cultures. The cage comprises many bars, each of which represents some characteristic of the individual's cultural background, life experiences or current context. Different bars are painted depending on their relevance to the point of view that is being shared, presented, or questioned (Figure 1.7).

During the dialog, when one participant *paints a bar* of his/her cage this can be visible to both participants, assuming that they are reflecting on the dialog. This reflection constitutes an internal dialog. This means that each participant may achieve some insight about himself or herself and simultaneously about the other participant (Figure 1.8.). The cage painting metaphor is significantly different from the two-way transmission process (encode/decode each way) described by Claude E. Shannon and Warren Weaver (1967) and the conduit metaphor (Reddy, 1979) of communication. Aside from considering the flow of communication in a different way, it also accounts for the way in which misunderstandings can be avoided or overcome through a process of making explicit the hidden effects of life experiences, cultural background and context on perspectives and consequently on communication.

During coconstruction of meaning and mutual understanding, a dialog is going on between the two people as they explore, reflect, and coreflect on their perspectives (Figure 1.8.). During the dialog several things are happening:

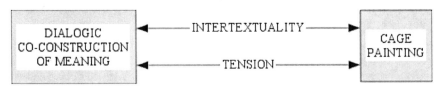

Figure 1.7. Cage painting metaphor: Intertextuality and tension relationships between the ground, dialogic coconstruction of meaning, and its topic, cage painting.

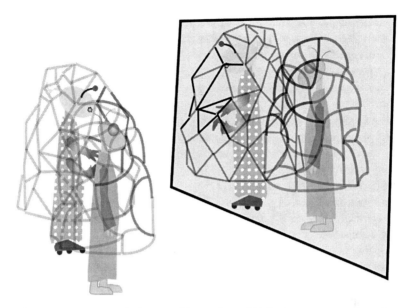

Figure 1.8.   Cage painting: An illustration of dialogic coconstruction of meaning and identity, inner dialog, reflection and coreflection.

(a) The person M says something to person G (it is shaped by M's cage)
(b) G interprets this (it passes through G's cage)
(c) G reflects

(a') The person G replies (says something) to person M (it is shaped by G's cage)
(b') M interprets this (it passes through M's cage)
(c') M reflects
(a") ...

For example, the person M from one place, where the weather is cool and dry, is visiting G, who lives far away in another place, where the weather is hot and humid. M is bothered by the humidity and wonders whether G realizes how uncomfortable it is for M.

— M asks G, "What do you think about the weather today?" [a]
— G has lived here a long time and loves the humidity. [b]
— G pauses to reflect on the fact that M's first question is about the weather and wonders why M has asked this question. [c]
— G responds, "I like it, how about you?" [a']
— M is impressed that G likes this weather [b']

— M reflects that this is an opportunity to share about what type of weather M is used to and how uncomfortable M is feeling, even though G seems to like the humidity. [c']

— M answers, "thanks for asking; actually I am finding the humidity very uncomfortable, because I live in a cool and dry climate." [a"]

In summary, the ongoing coreflection may be described as two intertwined processes: (1) interpretation of each other's contributions via their cages, and (2) reflection by each person on their perspective (through his/her cage)—inner dialog.

The act of copainting cage bars involves both negotiation of meaning about a cultural issue (represented by the bar) and achieving this while *saving face* on a mutual basis. This process requires ongoing reflection. The theories of identity negotiation and cross-cultural face-negotiation of Stella Ting-Toomey (1999) support this view. We can never entirely paint our own cage bars or those of the recipient; like the ongoing, never ending process of coconstructing cultural identity (Jensen, 2003). But, we can continue efforts for mutual understanding, keeping in mind existing constraints, some obvious (painted) and many invisible (not painted, yet). Our continued painting may reveal differences in the visibility of our bars both over time and depending on context. We may even recognize some incongruities within and among our own observed characteristics. The act of copainting cage bars is not only about building an understanding of others' perspectives. Rather, it is also about the processes that shaped the perspectives (perspective consciousness), and which may ultimately redefine our overall perspective.

> To understand another person's utterance means to orient oneself with respect to it, to find the proper place for it in the corresponding context. For each word of the utterance that we are in the process of understanding, we, as it were, lay down a set of our own answering words. The greater their number and weight, the deeper and more substantial our understanding will be.... *Any true understanding is dialogic in nature* [authors' emphasis]. Understanding is to utterance as one line of dialogue is to the next. (Voloshinov, 1929/1973, p. 102)

Satoshi Ishii's (1984) *Enryo-Sasshi* model is another way to illustrate copainting (Figure 1.9). William J. Starosta and Guo-Ming Chen (2005) used this model to emphasize the importance of time devoted to *listening*. Listening in their analysis includes the interpreting and shaping of messages.

In this model the *Enryo* stage involves the careful shaping of a message by a speaker G. The goal is twofold. On the one hand G conveys the

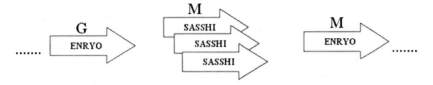

Figure 1.9.   One instance of the Enryo-Sasshi model.

intended meaning. On the other hand, G has to do it in such a way as to avoid offense to M. This will foster continuation of the dialog, saving face on both sides. During the *Sasshi* stage, when the listener, M, receives the message, he/she tries to decode the message to determine its original intended meaning and hence choose an appropriate interpretation. Once M has chosen from among alternative interpretations of G's intended meaning, M then enters the *Enryo* stage of shaping a response. This Enryo-Sasshi process of sending and decoding messages and active listening continues. This type of dialog may begin with a large gap between the meaning that G intends and the meaning that M is deducing. But after a number of iterations, the meanings will converge on a common understanding of some intercultural difference or similarity.

In our example after Figure 1.8, Enryo and Sasshi stages appear as follows:

Enryo (G):   Person G shapes the message (intrapersonal level) and then says something to person M
Sasshi (M):   M interprets this
M reflects
M considers alternatives
Enryo (M):   M replies to person G
Sasshi (G):   G interprets this
G reflects
G considers alternatives
Enryo (G):   …

Dialogic coconstruction of mutual understandings represented by the cage painting metaphor and partially illustrated by the Enryo-Sasshi model, can be considered an essential part of the intercultural and global communication competences. In the next section we present a model of global communication competences from the point of view of the cultural proficiency continuum and intercultural communication competences.

GLOBAL COMMUNICATION COMPETENCES

The two central components of intercultural *communication* are *culture* and communication and the two reference points are *environment* and *power relationships*. The central components and the reference points provide a setting for consideration of intercultural communication competences. The meaning of culture includes its construction through situated interactions. As culture is closely tied to communication, a contextual setting is closely intertwined with dialectic and dynamics of its power relationships. These two central components and the two reference points are used to capture, describe and theorize about related intercultural and global communication competences. While intercultural communication competences can be considered in any setting, from local to global, global communication competences refer to a set of abilities that assume *global mindset* and *global context*. The *glocal context* is beginning to mean global mindset and consequent actions in a local context. We will now consider in more detail these two communication competences and their relationship.

The following subsection, Cultural Proficiency Continuum, focuses on thoughtfulness about and appreciation of other cultures. It is followed by further consideration of intercultural and global communication competences.

Cultural Proficiency Continuum

[C]ulture hides much more than it reveals, and strangely enough what it hides it hides most effectively from its own participants.

Hall (1977, p. 51)

An understanding of the cultural proficiency continuum can be useful for examination of the individual's and group's recognition and attentiveness toward other cultures. Randall B. Lindsey, Kikanza Nuri Robins, and Raymond D. Terrell (2003) define a discrete number of levels in this continuum and provide tools for assessment of an individual's or group's current level. The cultural proficiency continuum model (Figure 1.10) consists of the following levels: cultural destructiveness; cultural incapability; cultural blindness; cultural precompetence; cultural competence; and cultural proficiency.

The essence of *cultural destructiveness* is the elimination of other people's cultures. For example, "This is Simealand, everyone should speak Simean!" or "All students in my class are the same to me, so I have never allowed any of my students to interrupt with questions in my class no

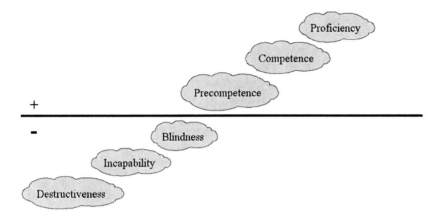

Figure 1.10. A person's position on cultural proficiency continuum is not fixed; it can vary dependent on person's familiarity with context and awareness of embedded power relationships

matter what!" At the next level, *cultural incapability* involves belief in the superiority of one's own culture and behavior that disempowers another's culture. For example, "Students from Simealand are not usually successful in my classes!" or "People from Simealand are the best in everything!" Further along the continuum is *cultural blindness*, which is characterized by acting as if the cultural differences do not matter; not recognizing that there are differences among and between cultures. For example, "When I see children with big noses, I do not see their nose or ears I only see children." Cultural *precompetence* is marked by an awareness of the limitations of one's skills when interacting with other cultural groups. An example is not supporting members of underrepresented groups after recruiting them into your workplace.

The *cultural competence* level involves keeping in mind the following sets of behaviors, when interacting with other cultural groups. In terms of cultural differences, these are (a) Honoring and respecting differences and (b) Attending to the dynamics of differences. In terms of one's cultural knowledge and values, behaviors include: (a) Continually reflecting on one's own culture; (b) Adapting one's values and behaviors; and (c) Expanding cultural knowledge and resources. Examples of culturally competent behaviors include, "We have some students from Simealand. We should check when they celebrate holidays from their home culture, so our picnics don't clash," or "We should study the culture of our incoming students to better differentiate instruction."

A *culturally proficient person* knows how to learn about other cultures and interacts effectively in a variety of cultural environments. Some behaviors that are exhibited by the culturally proficient individual include: welcoming and dealing with culturally disorienting dilemmas in a positive manner; valuing difference and diversity; conscientizing individual and group identity; facilitating the dynamics of diversity; mainstreaming cultural diversity; and changing for diversity (Lindsey et al., 2003).

This scale of cultural proficiency represents an advance on earlier scales, such as that of Alan J. Singerman (1996), which focuses on empathy toward other cultures and ability to observe and analyze other cultures at levels that are equivalent to precompetence, competence, and proficiency. The cultural proficiency continuum model differentiates levels below these—the negative levels. Julie A. Storme and Mana Derakhshani (2002), argue that it is just as important to understand lower level behaviors, such as those described by Christine Bennett (1993), or the three lower levels of cultural proficiency continuum: cultural destructiveness, cultural incapability, and cultural blindness (Lindsey et al., 2003). This information is useful for designing appropriate learning experiences to help people advance toward cultural competence and proficiency.

Assessing where a person is on the cultural proficiency continuum is not straightforward or simple. Whatever assessment method is used, it is very important to recognize that person can be at different levels of the continuum in different situations. Among the assessment methods that can help determine the proficiency level in a particular context are: responses to images or scenarios; role-plays; simulations; pie charts representing significance of aspects of identity; and text analysis of reflections. A combination of these would be needed to triangulate on the cultural proficiency continuum level and remove effects of the individuals trying to present themselves in an idealistic manner.

Intercultural Communication Competences

Intercultural competence is often understood to mean a combination of social and communicative skills that include: empathy; ability to work collaboratively and deal with conflict; respect for nonnative language speakers; techniques for handling misunderstanding and miscommunication; reflection on one's own cultural background; flexibility and tolerance for ambiguity. It is also important to realize that different cultures have particular discussion styles, speech rhythms, interpretation, and thought patterns (Liddicoat, 2002; Meyer, 2002).

Some scholars viewed intercultural communication competence as equivalent to or a function of communication effectiveness. The others conceptualized it from the perspective of appropriateness (Chen, 1989). Different approaches have been used to characterize intercultural communication effectiveness, all of them considering the *sojourner*. The sojourner's personality, world view, and cultural awareness formed the basis of one approach (e.g., Detweiler, 1975); observation of the sojourner's behavior in interactions was in the center of the second approach (e.g., Ruben & Kealey, 1979); while the third approach was more integrative (e.g., Gudykunst, Hammer, & Wiseman, 1977), examining both sojourner's characteristics and his/hers behavior in interactions. An ability to demonstrate a socially appropriate communication behavior in intercultural interactions requires individuals to make sense of messages while contextualizing them verbally, relationally and environmentally. *Verbal* contextualization points to the language, wording of statements and topics. *Relational* context requires certain agreement in terms of relationships developed through messages. Furthermore, individuals in interactions have to consider constraints imposed on their messages by the environment, and therefore *environmental* contextualization (Wiemann & Backlund, 1980). Contextualizing messages verbally, relationally, and environmentally is part of the cage painting process.

Chen (1989) synthesized from the literature a definition of intercultural communication competence that encompasses both effectiveness and appropriateness perspectives. His construct included a set of intercultural communication competence components clustered into four dimensions:

> *Personal attributes:* self-disclosure, self-awareness, self-concept and social relaxation;
> *Communication skills:* message skills, social skills, flexibility, interaction management;
> *Psychological adaptation:* frustration, stress, alienation, ambiguity; and
> *Cultural awareness:* social values, social customs, social norms, and social systems.

For the purposes of this book, it is important to notice that these dimensions and components are based mainly on the research that focused on the intercultural communication competence of sojourners, therefore giving a significant place to the psychological adaptation to another culture, which often involves overcoming a cultural shock. Further conceptualization was needed to account for both high mobility and the emergence of *global reach*. The latter is facilitated by availability of various communication technology tools and increased access to the Internet. Such analyses can be found in more recent works of many authors (e.g., Chen, 2005; Chen & Starosta, 2004). The following section deals with global communication competences. The following model of global communication competence was inspired by Chen's work and our own cultural and global experiences and knowledge.

Model of Global Communication Competences

Being able to understand and acknowledge the perspectives and experiences of others is an essential skill in communication. This improves the chances of a listener interpreting the ideas you are communicating as you intend. Developing and nurturing the human ability to *put oneself into another's shoes* or *see through the eyes of others* is challenging. It becomes even more challenging among people with very different cultural backgrounds, which is bound to happen more often in culturally diverse and global environments. *Seeing through the eyes of others*, being able to understand the other person's feelings within the scope of one's own identity, is one of the many metaphoric expressions of empathy. Expressing empathy is a process of recognizing the emotional side of others and understanding their perspective at a deeper level. It requires an understanding of the underlying values, beliefs and attitudes that define others' perspectives. Empathy may be considered an essential part of global communication competence. It can be *combined and interconnected* in different ways with other intercultural and global communication competences (e.g., Adams & Carfagna, 2006; Chen, 2005; Friedman, 2005). An individual with great empathy seems to be able to sense and react appropriately to other peoples' feelings, exhibit Enryo-Sasshi active listening, and interact in such a way as to establish great affinity with people of other cultures (Barnlund, 1988; Chen, 2005; Starosta & Chen, 2005).

The global communication competences may be considered as abilities to continuously revise and nurture one's: (a) cultural landscape, (b) dialectic interactions, and (c) global identity, all of which underpin one's *global mindset*.

Global Mindset

> *You must be the change you wish to see in the world.*
>
> —Mahatma Gandhi

A mindset is usually described as a way of thinking, based on a set of beliefs, which determines one's point of view or more generally a worldview. People said to have a *global mindset* have the ability to see the world from a broad perspective and are cognizant of emerging trends and opportunities. By being sensitive to the ways of other people, they are able to achieve personal balance through creatively blending their own characteristics or habits with those of other individuals. They are generally knowledgeable about and understanding of economic, cultural, social and political dimensions. They are systems thinkers, being able to see both the whole picture and being able to critically analyze components and their relationships. When combined, these characteristics allow them to adapt to new circumstances through a process of active dialog in which new meanings are negotiated and their identities evolve. In summary, a global mindset allows the individual to handle the complexities of the world. It includes components of the cultural landscape (e.g., cage) and dialectic world view. Chapter 3 will provide additional details about dialectic way of thinking about the world that surrounds us.

Lifelong Cage Painting: Continuously Revising One's Cultural Landscape.

The development of one's *cultural landscape* begins in early childhood within the family and grows with educational, social, travel, and other experiences. Our cultural landscape, which corresponds to our cage bars, comprises a continual and outwardly growing array of influences on the perspective we have of our own and other's cultures, a cultural patchwork. Our cultural landscape is dependent on our life experiences with people from other cultures. At one end of the spectrum, an individual's cultural landscape may be reflective of having lived in a homogeneous culture with minimal outside influences. How can such an individual advance in cultural proficiency beyond the level of cultural blindness? At the other end of the spectrum there are people, who have lived in several countries, who speak a number of languages and who have worked in more than one field. Their cultural landscape is likely to be much more complex. If we visualize that each patch of the landscape represents an influence on the person's cultural development, then a complex web of relationships connects these patches. During the individual's cultural development, the addition of a new patch may involve initial bewilderment and frustration with the new influence or encounter followed by the cognitive analysis and empathetic awareness that lead to immersion in the new culture (Chen, 2005). Such experiences may belong to the third place processes and we believe that they facilitate achievement of a higher level of cultural competence. Some of the individuals with such a background will enjoy and seek out diverse cultural experiences that enables them to improve his/hers cultural competence. The ability to continually revise their cultural landscape is closely related to their ability to see differences from the perspective of the other person's culture, a trait that Chen named, "empathic awareness" (p. 9).

Dialectic Interactions

Dialectic interactions between people in a global setting can be considered using the already mentioned framework: culture and communication; and context and power relationships (Martin &

Nakayama, 1999). The effectiveness and appropriateness (Chen, 1989), of such interactions needs to be considered in terms of making choices during global communication to achieve certain goals. These choices need to reflect the interactants' cultures, global contexts and power relationships. The capacity to negotiate multiple meanings and manage complexity and conflicts in the global context requires integration of cognitive and affective abilities. Dialectic thinking may support effective and appropriate facilitation of this process. Cage painting as a coreflective activity (Figure 1.8.) captures the dialectic nature of global interactions. To take the dialectic to the goal of understanding each other's perspective, one needs to actively listen, reflect, and employ a purposeful questioning strategy. This corresponds to the achievement of a *double-emic* perspective during intercultural communication (Starosta & Chen, 2005). The *Enryo-Sasshi* model (Ishii, 1984), (Figure 1.9) captures this dialectic process of shaping and sending messages (Enryo) and then interpreting messages while considering alternatives (Sasshi). Such a dialectic-based interaction may narrow the gap between their positions on an intercultural issue.

Negotiating Cultural Identity In Global Setting

To become a global citizen, one needs to nurture personal attitudes, values and beliefs about global identity in the global, national and local contexts. This includes professional, social and personal areas of life. It demands being knowledgeable about and understanding the economic, cultural, social and political dimensions in all of these contexts (across borders and cultures). This process of becoming a global citizen involves negotiating your perspective within the tension between globalization and individualization through an ongoing dialectic.

The *global* mind is one that contextualizes one's identity globally and adapts that identity internally. To accomplish that, individuals need to nurture and expand personal attributes of flexibility, sensitivity, creativity, open-mindedness, motivation, awareness of others' perspectives, and recognition of distinct representations (Adams & Carfagna, 2006; Chen, 2005; Langer, 1997; Nagata, 2006). Global communication competence also requires both intrapersonal and interpersonal abilities, being familiar with one's own inner states, and paying attention to the feelings of others (Taylor, 2000). Negotiating one's cultural identity in a global setting is a lifelong and autonomous learning process.

SUMMARY: WHERE WE ARE AND WHERE WE ARE GOING?

Our conception of global communication competences is reflective of (a) culture and identity being dynamic and complex and (b) intercultural interactions being based on a dialectic flow of thinking for dialogic coconstruction of mutual understandings. We used the language of metaphors to present the cage painting framework for conceptualizing successful intercultural communication. The cage and cage painting models add value to our understanding of intercultural and global communication development (see Figure 1.11). In chapter 2, we describe the cage painting learning environment as a setting for constructivist learning of the cage painting strategies. In chapter 3, we explore and discuss the theoretical framework that underlies and informs our approach to improving intercultural communication. A discussion of case studies and examples from different discipline areas in chapter 4 brings together concepts from the first three chapters and leads to an instructional blueprint for the design of cage painting and global learning environments.

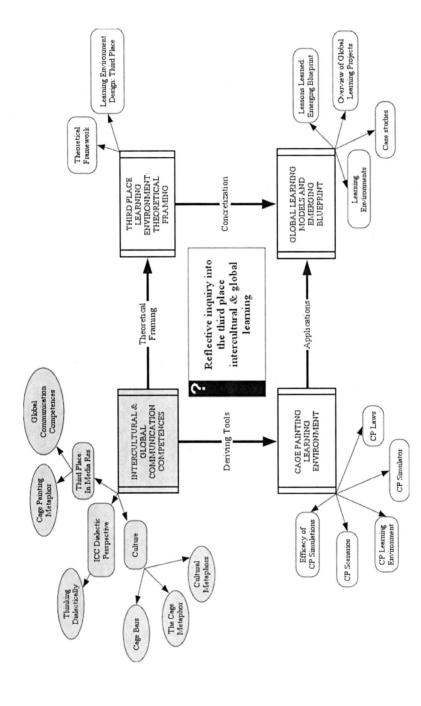

Figure 1.11. Constructing an understanding of intercultural and global communication competence.

CHAPTER 2

CAGE PAINTING
LEARNING ENVIRONMENT

INTRODUCTION

Learning intercultural communication would proceed better if it proceeded through relatively complex and carefully constructed simulations of culturally embedded institutional talk contexts, and focused not on rules but on strategies and critique.

Young (1996, p. 182)

Intercultural/global communication competence underpins successful interaction between culturally diverse groups at a local/urban level as well as communication within globally distributed, multicultural teams. This chapter explores how intercultural communication (ICC) on an individual level can be improved through simulation exercises and how this can serve as preparation for communication in both culturally diverse local and global learning environments.

In the first section of this chapter we (a) illustrate how literature and role play-based and computer simulation approaches can provide useful preparation for intercultural interactions, and (b) consider critical issues related to the degree of transfer of the strategies to real-life contexts. This supports the notion of the cage painting learning environment (CPLE), which encompasses Web-based, role-play simulations, whose design is based on

Third Place Learning: Reflective Inquiry Into Intercultural and Global Cage Painting
pp. 33–67
Copyright © 2008 by Information Age Publishing

the cage painting metaphor. In the second section a scenario template for cage painting simulations is introduced. Its inherent characteristic is an underpinning ICC heuristic. The scaffolding within templates guides the learner to conceptualize a heuristic to benefit his/her ICC. The overall CPLE is described in terms of (a) the embedded learning processes, (b) the contextualized situation, and (c) cognitive apprenticeship. The cage painting simulator (CPS) interface, part of the CPLE, and its associated scenario repository are described in the next section. The data-generation feature of the CPLE, which allows it to be used to study the nature of learners' ICC development, is also described.

THE EFFICACY OF CAGE PAINTING SIMULATIONS

The Need for Cage Painting Tool

One significant challenge of working in globally distributed, multicultural teams stems from time zone differences (Figure 2.1). In the teaching environment, additional issues include the lack of alignment of the starting and finishing dates of semesters and the timing of religious or other holidays (Figure 2.2). Together, these constraints limit the windows of opportunity for global interactions. The nature and frequency of interactions depend on the characteristics of groups that are interacting. In most cases synchronous sessions such as video conferences will be infrequent compared with asynchronous sessions that use threaded discussions or e-mail.

Therefore the amount of time available for synchronous communication is short and the pressure to collaborate and achieve goals is high. Collaborating under such conditions increases the probability that communication will be affected by cultural and other preconceptions or even disorienting dilemmas. This illustrates the need to prepare participants so they could make the best use of the limited time for direct communication. The best preparation, next to real-life experiences, is to provide them with a conceptual framework for improving ICC strategies that is integrated into some role-play simulations. This led to the idea of the Web-based, role-play simulations based on the cage painting metaphor and integrated into the CPLE.

The cage painting simulations that are provided in the CPLE are used to help learners conceptualize and visualize the process of developing ICC competence by improving an understanding of their own perspective—painting the bars of their own cage—and gaining an understanding of the perspective of others with different cultural backgrounds—painting the bars of the other's cage. This process involves dialogic negotiation of

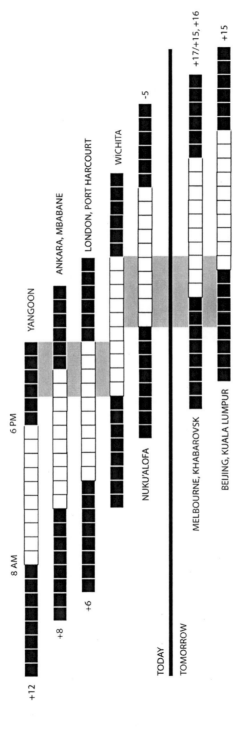

Figure 2.1. Time zone differences between Wichita and other locations.

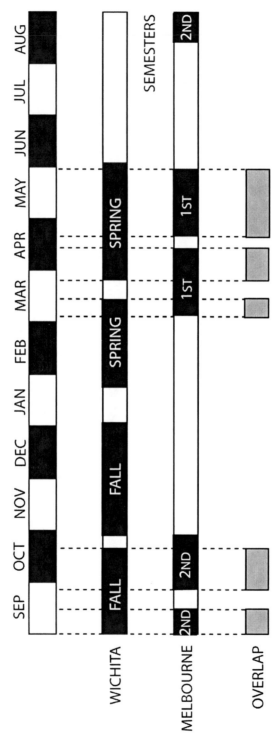

Figure 2.2.   Lack of semester alignment between Wichita and Melbourne: black represents semesters for each location; overlap periods are shown in gray.

meaning and identity, which metaphorically is akin to both participants holding the paintbrush as they paint their respective cages. This simultaneous cage painting is a form of self-discovery and of understanding the other's perspective; it is reciprocated during the process.

A critical issue in the design and implementation of the CPS is how effective it is in terms of transfer; how what is learned in the simulated learning context can be applied in real-life contexts. In the next section we explore the process of transfer from different contexts for learning, such as reading intercultural literature, role-plays, and simulation games, such as CPS. Some clues from the literature about transfer of the learning outcomes accomplished using fiction and media apply equally to simulation and can inform the development and application of CPS.

TRANSFER: FROM LEARNING CONTEXT TO TARGET CONTEXT

Transfer of knowledge refers to applying existing knowledge in another context. To develop competence in ICC, one must be able to organize related knowledge in ways that facilitate its retrieval and application. Organizing this information into a conceptual framework facilitates the process of transfer (National Research Council, 2000). In the context of ICC development, there are multiple ways of conceptualizing available sources, such as appropriate literature and role-playing.

To improve intercultural competence, Frampton Fox (2003) presented an approach based on the use of literary accounts that provide insights into other cultures: "Intercultural competences can be better achieved by evoking the imagination of the culture learner through the vicarious experience afforded through good fiction" (p. 99). The contextualization found in the literature stimulates imagination and visualization. It helps to reduce the gap between the learning and real-life contexts (Figure 2.3). Even members of the same culture, ethnicity, and gender may approach intercultural learning from different perspectives and with different preferred learning styles. Purposeful use of literature can supplement learning outcomes of

Figure 2.3.   The transfer distance between the learning context and target context: from far transfer (literature) through imagination/visualization and CPS to near transfer (role play).

role-play and help as a bridge in the transfer of learning to real experience. Furthermore, having the opportunity to compare and contrast virtual experiences with the literature can help reduce anxiety and increase sensitivity of the learner concerning the real experience.

Similar to Frampton Fox's (2003) illustrations, the cage painting simulations may also serve as a mechanism for coping with culture shock or disorienting dilemmas in the context of another culture. This coping may occur at the level of point of view where a simple analysis of the situation helps clarify a preconception or misunderstanding. More challenging is a situation that requires deeper examination of the participants' beliefs and attitudes. Learning via the simulations allows this examination to occur while remaining in the comfort of the learner's home culture.

The version of CPS described in this book uses a simulated interactive chat interface, rather than the full richness of a highly graphical computer game. This apparent limitation in fact provides an advantage. Without the graphics and having only words to convey meaning, the imagination of the learners is stimulated in a different way. No two learners will necessarily visualize or imagine the virtual context in the same way. This adds to the richness of the approach. It is similar to *the book is better than the movie* effect due to the limitations of rendering a rich piece of literature into the cinematic domain.

The pedagogical approach presented here is a shift from the banking model, described by Jerold W. Apps (1991, p. 23) as the *bucket filling* approach, to one that evokes curiosity and conscientization (Freire, 1968/ 1970). It supports learning for understanding (Perkins & Unger, 1999). Just as engaging intercultural literature may stimulate critical reflection for the learner, so too will well-formulated CPS scenarios centered on resolving misunderstandings. In addition, connecting to the learner's prior knowledge and experience will increase its cognitive and emotional significance and thus improve the transfer. The transfer of what is learned from the CPS and other activities to the target context, such as an intercultural/global learning environment, can be improved through attention to underlying conditions and mechanisms.

Transfer Distance

The ultimate aim of education is to empower learners to be able to transfer what they learned in some *learning context* to a *target context* (Figure 2.3). The CPS is the learning context and the target context could be an interaction between two people of different cultures, face-to-face or via communication technology. The transfer may be a *near transfer* between two similar contexts, such as from one English-speaking country to another or a *far transfer*, for example, between China and Sweden. Each transfer can be said to have a *transfer distance*. Along the transfer distance (Figure 2.3), there are examples of learning activities, such as: (a) reading literature about another culture, both fiction and nonfiction; (b) *visualization* or *imagination* that this invokes; (c) *simulation* or *role-playing*; and finally (d) *experiences* interacting with people of another culture. The topic of this chapter is the use of simulation as preparation for real-life experiences. The transfer literature suggests that a balance of specific examples and general principles may promote the most effective transfer (National Research Council, 2000). David N. Perkins and Gavriel Salomon (1992) list five catalysts for transfer: metaphors or analogies, thorough and diverse practice, explicit abstraction, arousing mindfulness, and active self-monitoring (Figure 2.4).

The specific cage painting simulations are based on the cage painting metaphor discussed in chapter 1. The lack of understanding of an individual's culture or that of others is represented as an invisible cage, which needs to be *painted* to improve communication. This metaphor helps the learner to conceptualize the process of improving the understanding of their own culture and that of others. The CPS helps broaden and deepen the information base about communication and the development of a related conceptual framework, which in turn will support transfer to new situations (National Research Council, 2000). As learners play different simulations and later write scenarios for new simulations, they are provided with diverse practice. While the learner plays a series of increasingly difficult scenarios, they may start to develop strategies—*general principles*—that can then apply to future simulation scenarios and/or to real experience. An important part of learning with the CPS is to reflect on which

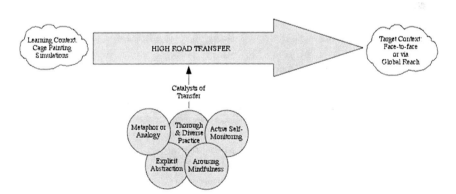

Figure 2.4. From cage painting simulations to the intercultural/global learning environment: three mechanisms and five catalysts for transfer.

strategies have worked and which have not. This can be facilitated with appropriate guiding reflective questions. The combination of developing strategies and reflection-in-action (Schön, 1987) will lead to a more mindful state, or awareness of self and context.

David N. Perkins and Gavriel Salomon (1992) discussed two significantly different transfer mechanisms: *Mindful* or *high-road* and *low-road* transfer (Figure 2.4). High road transfer requires abstraction and a search for connections where knowledge can be applied. Low-road transfer refers to semiautomatic application of knowledge, such as in the use of stereotypes (Dodd, 1998). It relates to skills or competences that are used in reaction to a situation similar to that in which the skills or competences were developed. Therefore, high(er) road transfer requires a higher degree of mindfulness than low-road transfer (Schunk, 2004).

Transfer related to CPS is mainly high road transfer. It requires mindful abstraction and recognition of a situation in which learned strategies can be applied. The example of two groups of students learning to throw darts at targets at the bottom of a pool of water (National Research Council, 2000, p. 18) illustrates the role of abstraction—in that case understanding refraction—as a mechanism for transfer from a pool of one depth to another. Students with abstract understanding were able to transfer to the new situation, whereas those without it had difficulty.

As factors affecting transfer from the learning context to a target context are analyzed for the CPS, it is helpful to compare this learning context with others, such as role-plays or use of the intercultural literature.

Role-Plays

Stepping into someone else's shoes is an age-old way of learning that is more effective than merely hearing third-hand about another person's circumstances or life experiences. Role-play provides an engaging and experiential method of learning about a topic at more depth. This approach has been used, for example, in model United Nations simulations in K-12 classes and in higher education (Shaw, 2004). Meanwhile with the advent of online learning, a common deficiency is the lack of focus on interactivity between participants (e.g., Harasim, Hilz, Teles, & Turoff, 1995). Online role-play is not new. It was facilitated with the development of multiuser role-playing games, for example, MUDs (multiuser domain), and object-oriented MUDs (Wills & Ip, 2002), *The Palace* (Suler, 1999) and more recently *Second Life* (Herman, Coombe, & Kaye, 2006). Online role-plays may have some advantages over face-to-face role-plays with physical copresence, namely being anonymous and asynchronous (Bell, 2001; Chester & Gwynne, 1998; Freeman & Capper, 1999).

Participating in a role-play by interacting with a synthetic character, rather than interacting with another person, extrapolates upon the idea of online role-play simulation. It provides an opportunity to more tightly scaffold progress toward specific learning goals. The learner can be confronted by a preconception in introductory simulations and then as he or she derives strategies, he/she can advance to more challenging disorienting dilemmas. It is important that the scenarios are not specific to a real culture, so as to avoid players lapsing into the use of stereotyping. This will ensure transfer of ability to deal with preconceptions or disorienting dilemmas of *any* culture.

Fiction-Intercultural Literature

When can the intercultural literature, such as *Letters Back to Ancient China* (Rosendorfer, 1997), be useful in providing signposts for intercultural competence? Transfer from the context of reading the literature of other cultures can be enhanced through careful choice of readings. Guided reflection can help the reader to identify specific competences. Frampton Fox (2003, Table 1, p. 106) lists in a comparative manner cultural competences provided by Carley H. Dodd (1998), Muriel I. Elmer (1986), Daniel J. Kealey (2000) and William B. Gudykunst (1998).

Practicing and applying ICC is an active process of negotiating meaning during which the learner transforms his/her perspective in order to understand and accommodate the culture of others (Taylor, 1994). The authors mentioned above—William B. Gudykunst, Carley H. Dodd, Muriel I. Elmer, Daniel J. Kealey—all agree that *tolerance for ambiguity* is a common indicator of ICC competence along with an orientation toward people rather than tasks, plus interpersonal skills, empathy, self-confidence, and being positive.

Being positive in thought—cognitively—is linked with a positive emotional outlook, which stimulates better interactions and outcomes (Burns, 1980). In choosing particular works of fiction from the intercultural literature, attention needs to be given to the degree to which the work evokes the learner's emotions, or engages the learner at an emotional level. The ideal novel will trigger the reader's imagination to adopt the perspective of one or more characters. This can be achieved through description of the environment or situations that are convincingly those of someone not familiar with a cultural context. In *Letters back to Ancient China*, Rosendorfer (1997) presented the perspective of a person transported in a time machine from the ancient capital, Kai-feng of the early Northern Song dynasty in the tenth century in China, to modern-day Ming-chen (Kao-tai's pronunciation of Munich), Germany. The impressions of common objects or daily occurrences in Munich by the character, Kao-tai, from the perspective of a court poet from 1,000 years earlier in China causes the reader to wonder and speculate what he was describing.

> I heard an unimaginable roaring, grinding, rattling noise approach; there is simply no comparison for it in our world. At the same time a huge animal— or a fiery demon, that was the thought that flashed through my mind—came rushing towards me at lightning speed. (p. 17)

For example, the above passage triggers uncertainty and possible fear for Kao-tai's safety in the mind of the reader. However, Kao-tai was referring to something we are used to seeing every day—a car in which the driver was avoiding running over Kao-tai, who is unwittingly standing in the middle of the road. On realizing this, the reader's emotion may move from apprehension to mirth as they realize how funny Kao-tai's description of a car was. In another example, later in the book, Kao-tai is writing to his friend Dji-gu, "I saw a grey iron dragon flying overhead at a low height. It was flying calmly, majestically, its head stretched out in front, its wings spread wide, gliding rather than flying" (Rosendorfer, 1997, p. 192) as a description of an aircraft. This later description is less filled with foreboding than the description of the car, because by now, after four months, Kao-tai is more used to seeing such things in the world of modern day Munich. Aside from these superficial descriptive elements, there is reflective discussion by Kao-tai in his letters to Dji-gu about contrasts such as the value system of modern-day Munich that puts more emphasis on consumerism and profit than in ancient China. On the other hand, it should be remembered that Kao-tai has come from a position of privilege, not having to continually compete to increase his status as reflected in overt possession of capital.

Another desirable quality in works of intercultural literature is exposure of the reader to different phases in the process of becoming more competent in understanding intercultural experiences. It is helpful for the reader to be taken systematically from being an outsider of a culture to becoming an insider and in the process illustrating the pattern of adaptation (Fox, 2003). Tom J. Lewis and Robert E. Jungman (1986) identified six phases of the intercultural experience, namely: preliminary, spectator, increasing participation, shock, adaptation, and reentry. The short stories in Lewis and Jungman's book are grouped according to these categories while other, longer stories, such as *Letters Back to Ancient China*, step through the phases.

The *preliminary* phase is characterized by anticipation and apprehension most likely based on preconceptions about the other culture. Kao-tai experienced some misgivings about going into future Kai-feng. At the beginning of his experience is a period of being an observer, the *spectator* phase, in which interpretations are colored by preconceptions that are not yet corrected, preconceptions rooted in prior knowledge and experiences. Kai-feng of the future does not fit within his frame of reference. He thinks, "[t]he future is an abyss.... Not even the darkest chaos is comparable to what lies in wait for the human race ... I feel as if I have been cast out into an indescribably cold, alien place" (Rosendorfer, 1997, p. 8). As interaction with members of the other culture begins, *increasing participation*, Kao-tai lets go of his prior self-conception by learning about the other culture. He tangles with the authorities after the car accident, but is befriended by Mr. Shi-shmi (Kao-tai's pronunciation of Schmidt) from whom he gradually learns more about local culture.

As this continues, there is an accumulation of differences that eventually cause a sense of *shock*, which according to Tom J. Lewis and Robert E. Jungman (1986) is accompanied by feelings of depression, withdrawal, isolation, and eccentric or compulsive behavior. For example, "Through most of his [a character newly arrived in India] experience of the rains, he was chronically and depressingly off colour. Whatever he ate turned his bowels to water. In such circumstances a human being goes short of courage" (Scott, 1979, p. 245). As the intercultural experience continues, the stranger starts to feel less like an outsider and *adapts* so he or she is able to express thoughts from the perspective of first and second and other cultures.

After adapting to another culture and then returning to the first culture—*reentry*—there is a period of reverse culture shock. This is due in part to adapting back to the first culture, and after a long period of absence, having to adapt back to things that have changed. A simple example is returning to find that there are new laws or the price of certain goods has increased.

CAGE PAINTING SCENARIOS

At the core of the CPS is a repository of simulations, each of which is generated from a cage painting scenario. Each scenario presents the player with a different context, contextual goal(s) and the challenge of overcoming a misunderstanding caused by a preconception or a disorienting dilemma. The underlying structure of the scenarios has four steps corresponding to four increasingly complex strategies. They can be used to resolve a given misunderstanding. The main goal for the learner, as he/she plays simulations, is to conceptualize four strategies well enough to both write new scenarios and use these strategies in real-life situations. Scenarios are just complex enough to allow the player to learn and practice the strategies, but simple enough to make it possible for the more experienced user to write new scenarios (Alagic, Gibson, & Rimmington, 2007; Rimmington, Gibson, & Alagic, 2007).

Underlying Structure of Cage Painting Scenarios

Every cage painting simulation is generated from a scenario undergirded by an ICC heuristic. An associated learning cycle and three types of feedback form an underlying structure for the collection of cage painting scenarios.

ICC Heuristic

During a CP simulation the learner is presented with opportunities to use four strategies, one for each cage painting level (CPL) represented in Figure 2.5. The first two are concerned with asking for and sharing each other's perspective:

Figure 2.5.   The ICC heuristic undergirding every cage painting scenario.

CPL1: Ask for the other's perspective.
CPL2: Offer a self-critical perspective.

The second two are more challenging and require adopting the perspective of the other when sharing and asking questions in such a way that the other person answers in your own perspective.

CPL3: Present self in terms of other's perspective.
CPL4: Ask a question to elicit an answer in your own perspective.

If the learner correctly chooses these strategies, he/she learns critical information for resolving a misunderstanding. Learning these strategies for dealing with communication challenges can be likened to climbing a staircase (Figure 2.5). Sometimes in a simulation scenario, the learner will make it to just the first level. Later, as the learner reiterates the learning cycle (Figure 2.6) and further acquire the ICC heuristic, he or she can reach higher levels for increasingly difficult scenarios (Alagic, Gibson, & Rimmington, 2007; Rimmington, Gibson, & Alagic, 2007).

First Learning Cycle

The learner can gain some virtual *concrete* experience by playing a CP simulation (Figure 2.6). As the learner plays the simulation, he/she can

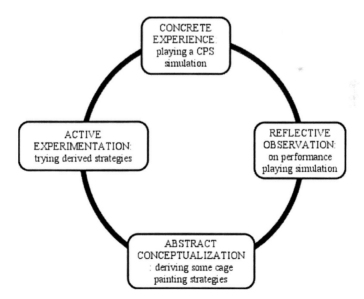

Figure 2.6.   Learning cycle associated with cage painting scenario-generated simulations.

reflect-in-action or reflect afterward about his/her performance and his/her success or lack of it. The feedback is designed so that learners: (a) can apply the strategies in further simulations for different scenarios; and (b) develop a heuristic (Figure 2.5.) that will aid their intercultural interactions.

Feedback

To facilitate the process in which the learner may conceptualize the ICC heuristic three types of feedback are provided:

— Coaching, about the CPLs associated with ICC heuristic, by the virtual character, Simea;
— Hints that indicate if the learner is making a good choice at each CPL; and
— Visual representation of Simea's and learner's cages being *painted* during the interactions/simulation.

Simea, the synthetic character with which the learner interacts, is of an unknown cultural background. She begins each scenario with a greeting and an initial question that opens the conversation. Then after the user makes a choice, Simea provides an appropriate response to good, mediocre or bad choices. Dialog continues with Simea acting as a mentor/coach for the learner by offering encouragement in the direction of the intended cage painting strategies. Even in the case of the learner being at the lowest level of the staircase (Figure 2.5) at the last step of a simulation, Simea still prompts the learner to choose a response that will help him or her to reach CPL4. In addition, the learner is provided with hints that indicate whether he or she is making a good choice (Figure 2.7). The third form of feedback is provided by cages: one for the learner's character and one for Simea's character. If the learner is making good choices then both cages darken (Figure 2.7). For mediocre choices, one or the other cage will darken, and in the case of bad choices there is no change to the cages. Dark cages indicate that barriers have become visible and communication can take that into account; dark cages at the end of a simulation provide feedback that the learner has been making *good* choices to advance up the CPLs.

Scenario Template

Cage painting scenario template is based on the underlying structure of cage painting scenarios (Figure 2.8). The template:

— Presents the learner—scenario designer—with four steps, each being a level of cage painting (CPL1 to CPL4);

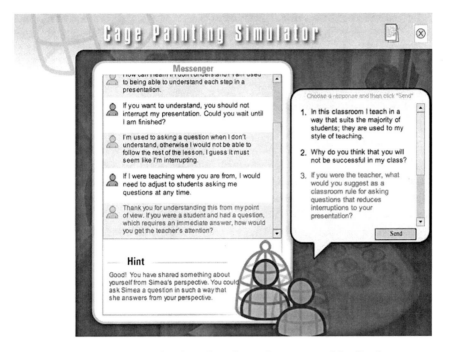

Figure 2.7. Cage painting simulator interface: Three types of feedback.

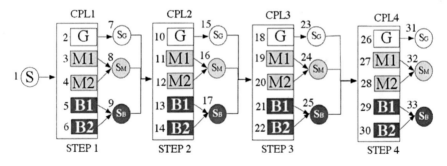

Figure 2.8. Template structure: (a) the four steps/CP levels; (b) [G]ood, [M]edio-cre and [B]ad choices at every level; and (c) corresponding responses by [S]imea, S_G, S_M, and S_B.

— Allows for three types of choices and associated responses (good, mediocre, and bad);

— Provides scaffolding to help the learner make progress with ICC development;

— Makes it easy for the scenario author to create; and

— At each of four steps, the learner is presented with five choices, one good (G), two mediocre (M1, M2), and two bad (B1, B2) (Figure 2.8).

Cage Painting Scenario Design: An Example

Each CP scenario has a topic, authors, underlying context and goal(s), and importantly, a cultural misunderstanding precipitated by a preconception that needs to be clarified (Figure 2.9a). This is accomplished by dialog between the learner and Simea. During this conversation the learner may choose contributions to the discussion that help with clarification of the preconception (good choices) or they may choose to make neutral statements (mediocre choices) or unhelpful statements (bad choices). The first CPL, out of four CPLs, involves asking questions about Simea's perspective on the relevant topic in response to Simea's initial greeting that includes a question (Alagic, Gibson, & Rimmington, 2007; Rimmington, Gibson, & Alagic, 2007). Figures 2.9a-f present an example of a scenario embedded within a template that has prompts for the author, scenario designer.

Simea's Initial Greeting

In the *Eye Contact* scenario (Figures 2.9a-f), the prompt for the author: *Pose a question that prompts the learner to ask something about Simea's perspective* is captured by Simea's question, "Why do you look at my eyes?" It is important to keep in mind that Simea is both a person of some other, unknown culture with whom the learner must negotiate a shared understanding and Simea acts to some extent as a role model and coach. She fulfills these roles by relying on CPL strategies and reminding the learner of what he/she needs to do to catch up to the current CPL level, even if the learner has made no progress by the fourth step.

Asking for Simea's Perspective: CPL1

After Simea has offered her initial greeting, the learner is presented with five choices. Each choice follows the prompts for the author, such as "Model CPL1: Ask for Simea's perspective" (Figure 2.9b). The author only needs to enter choices in the left-hand fields. Generic feedback provided in the right-hand fields will appear in the Hint box of the Interface (Figure 2.7). So the right-hand fields do not need to be modified. Choices should be about the same length, so as not to provide visual cues for the learner (Figure 2.9c).

Learning Scenario Topic: | Look Into My Eyes!

Describe the nature of the situation, including the place, the time, the learner's role and the role of Simea.

Setting and Context:

After competing at the Olympics, Simea is visiting with the person who has won the gold. Simea is not used to making eye contact with the person she speaks with and is feeling nervous because the other person is looking at her while talking. Whereas the other person likes to make eye contact when visiting, because it is a sign that they are paying attention.
AUTHORS OF THE SCENARIO: Larry, Linda and Cindy

Describe something about the cultural dissonance that the learner will experience in the scenario. It should be described in such a way that the misconception causing the dissonance is not immediately obvious. Present the goal that the learner needs to achieve through an intercultural dialog with Simea.

Challenge and Goal:

Nonverbal communication can be as meaningful as verbal. Your goal is to effectively communicate your customs with Simea without abandoning your cultural norms.

Simea's Initial Greeting

Prompt for the Author: Greeting. Pose a question that prompts the learner to ask something about Simea's perspective (CPL1).

Hi, my name is Simea. Why do you look into my eyes? Direct eye contact makes me nervous.

Figure 2.9a.   Learning scenario topic, setting and context, challenge and goal, and Simea's initial greeting with a prompt for the author.

STEP 1: Cage Painting Level One – Ask for Simea's Perspective

Good: **Prompt for the Author:** Return greeting. Answer Simea's question. Model CPL1: Ask for Simea's perspective.

> Buena Simea. Nice to meet you. How do I make you nervous when looking at you?

Prompt for the Author: Confirm their CPL1 choice is good and then prompt for CPL2.

> Good! You asked for Simea's perspective. You could also share your own perspective.

Mediocre: **Prompt for the Author:** Return greeting. Make a non-offensive statement or observation.

> Buena Simea. I did not realize that it makes you nervous when somebody looks at you.

Prompt for the Author: Acknowledge their choice, remind them of CPL1 and prompt for CPL2.

> You made an observation, but you should have asked for Simea's perspective. You could also share your own perspective.

Mediocre: **Prompt for the Author:** Return greeting. Make a non-offensive statement or observation.

> Buena Simea. I realize when talking to you that you try to avoid my eyes.

Prompt for the Author: Acknowledge their choice, remind them of CPL1 and prompt for CPL2.

> You made an observation, but you should have asked for Simea's perspective. You could also share your own perspective.

Bad: **Prompt for the Author:** Making an impolite statement, because you are generalizing from your limited experince about Simea and Simea's culture (from your own perspective).

> I realize when talking to you that you blush. I guess you are embarrassed about your loss.

Prompt for the Author: Share consequences of their bad choice. Remind them of CPL1 and prompt for CPL2.

> You may hurt Simea's feelings. It would be better to ask for Simea's perspective. You could also share your perspective.

Bad: **Prompt for the Author:** Making an impolite statement, because you are generalizing from your limited experince about Simea and Simea's culture (from your own perspective).

> I would be nervous too, if I were you and meeting the world champion. What are you, a loser?

Prompt for the Author: Share consequences of their bad choice. Remind them of CPL1 and prompt for CPL2.

> You may hurt Simea's feelings. It would be better to ask for Simea's perspective. You could also share your perspective.

Figure 2.9b. CPL1: Learner's choices, corresponding hints, and prompts for the author. After Simea has offered her initial greeting, the learner is presented with five choices.

Simea's Response to a Good Choice:

Prompt for the Author: Simea models the sharing of her culture and ask a clarifying question.

I am not comfortable with somebody who tries to look in my eyes. In my country it is insulting to a person to look into their eyes.

Simea's Response to a Mediocre Choice:

Prompt for the Author: Simea empathizes and asks a clarifying question (models CPL1) prompting for CPL2. She models CPL: by sharing about her culture in more detail.

Yes, of course. You are insulting me by looking at me constantly! Why are you constantly looking at me?

Simea's Response to a Bad Choice:

Prompt for the Author: Simea's reaction is defensive, but she still accomodates through a clarifying question.

I know that you are famous but that gives you no right to think you are better than everyone else. In my culture we do not look into each other's eyes and I am not used to that. Why does your culture use direct eye contact?

Figure 2.9c. CPL1: Simea's responses and prompts for the author.

Prompt for the Author: Answer Simea's question. Model CPL2: Share something about the learner's perspective.

> That is interesting. In my country you must look into somebody's eyes when having a conversation, otherwise you appear impolite.

Prompt for the Author: Simea models both learning points 1 and 2 by sharing her perspective and asking more about your perspective.

> People constantly look at each other. Do you not get nervous when talking, especially to somebody you hardly know?

Prompt for the Author: Confirm their CPL2 choice is good and then prompt for CPL3.

> Good! You shared something about your perspective. You could share something about yourself, but from Simea's perspective.

Figure 2.9d. CPL2: Good choice, Simea's response for a Good choice, the corresponding hint and prompts for the author.

Prompt for the Author: Model CPL3: Share something about the learner but from Simea's perspective in response to Simea's comment.

> If somebody does not feel comfortable talking in front of others, you would avoid looking at him or her straight in the eyes.

Prompt for the Author: Simea models learning point 3 by sharing her perspective and asking more about the user's perspective.

> I guess it is sometimes hard to check whether the other person is really listening or not. However, you must listen to his or her responses and could check his or her attention this way. Do you only decide depending on the eye-contact if a person is listening?

Prompt for the Author: Confirm their CPL3 choice is good and then prompt for CPL4.

> Good! You have shared something about yourself from Simea's perspective. You could ask Simea a question in such a way that she answers from your perspective.

Figure 2.9e.   CPL3: Good choice, Simea's response to a Good choice, corresponding hint, and prompts for the author.

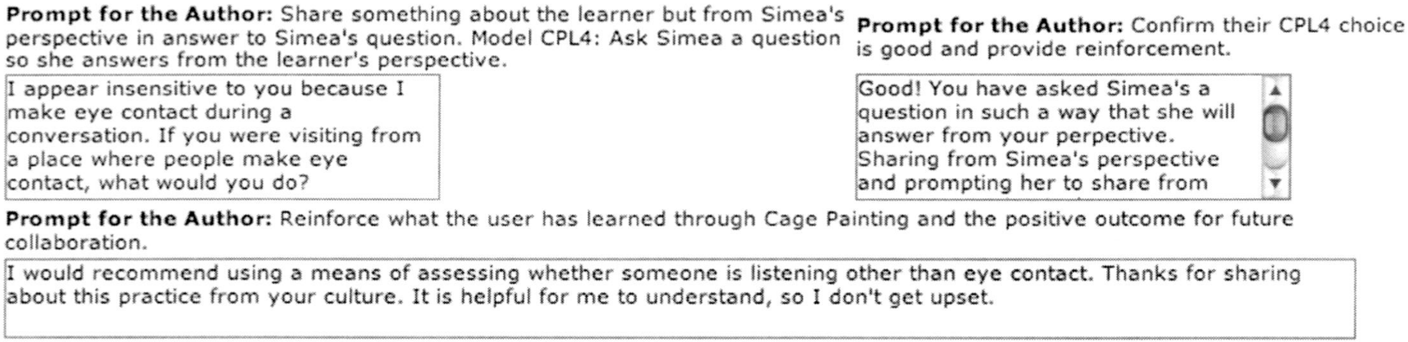

Prompt for the Author: Share something about the learner but from Simea's perspective in answer to Simea's question. Model CPL4: Ask Simea a question so she answers from the learner's perspective.

> I appear insensitive to you because I make eye contact during a conversation. If you were visiting from a place where people make eye contact, what would you do?

Prompt for the Author: Reinforce what the user has learned through Cage Painting and the positive outcome for future collaboration.

> I would recommend using a means of assessing whether someone is listening other than eye contact. Thanks for sharing about this practice from your culture. It is helpful for me to understand, so I don't get upset.

Prompt for the Author: Confirm their CPL4 choice is good and provide reinforcement.

> Good! You have asked Simea's a question in such a way that she will answer from your perpective. Sharing from Simea's perspective and prompting her to share from

Figure 2.9f.   CPL4: Good choice, Simea's response to a Good choice, corresponding hint, and prompts for the author.

The author needs to prepare responses by Simea to the learner's Good, Mediocre, and Bad choices for CPL1. Again the *Prompt for the Author* in each field makes it explicit what the author needs to include.

Presenting a Self-Critical Perspective: CPL2

CPL2 requires reflection on and evaluation of one's own perspectives in terms of the current situation in order to clarify one's perspective. Both Simea and the learner are expected to share this self-critical perspective (Figure 2.9d).

Presenting Self in Terms of Other's Perspectives: CPL3

In addition to being able to reflect on one's own perspective for the purpose of overcoming the cultural misunderstanding and clarifying the preconception, it is important to be able to reflect on a higher level from another's perspective. In this example (Figure 2.9e) for the Good choice the authors have put a proposition from Simea's point of view about avoiding eye contact during a conversation. Simea responds by offering a solution that from the learner's perspective emphasizes active listening rather than making eye contact.

Questioning to Elicit an Answer in Your Perspective: CPL4

Answering a question about the other's perspective or sharing your self-critical perspective requires reflecting on the current situation. Eliciting another's answer on the issue in your perspective is a challenge that requires both cognitive and metacognitive effort. In this scenario (Figures 2.9a-f) the CPL4 strategy "Ask Simea a question so she answers from your perspective" (Figure 2.9f) is modeled by the learner's question, "I appear insensitive to you because I make eye contact during a conversation. If you were visiting from a place where people make eye contact, what would you do?"

Care needs to be taken in the language of the scenario not to lapse into the use of stereotypes. That represents a major challenge for authors of scenarios since it is natural for everyone to judge things from their own perspective, based on their cultural identity, and they tend to provide explanations colored by that perspective. Notice in the CPL4 example the word *place* is used, rather than country. This is also consistent with Simea being from an unknown culture. The learner does need to pay close attention to making Good choices at CPL1 and CPL2 in order to achieve the level of understanding of the basis of the preconception so a Good choice can be made at CPL4. In real intercultural exchanges, the interactants may spend more time cycling through CPL1 and CPL2 exchanges before they have enough information to start constructing CPL3 and CPL4 perspectives and questions.

It is important to give some consideration to the transition from *ethnocentricity* to *ethnorelativism* (Bennett, 1986, 1993) in the context of progressing through the CPLs. The ability to present a self-critical appraisal of one's own cultural perspective (Figure 2.9d) is a step beyond the states of: *denial* in which other cultures are not acknowledged, *defense* in which one's own culture is regarded as superior and *minimization* in which differences between other cultures and one's own culture are trivialized. The ability to present one's self in terms of the perspective of others and to frame questions in such a way that the person from another culture reciprocates by answering as though from your perspective, enables the ethnorelative stages of acceptance, adaptation, and integration. *Acceptance* involves the realization that one's own culture is just one of many complex worldviews, while *adaptation* begins the process to imbibe the perceptions and behaviors of other cultures. Finally, Bennett's (1986) *integration* stage involves the ability to conceptualize the possibility of multiple perspectives, to move in and out of many different world views, or global *neonomadism* (Rimmington, Gibson, Gibson, & Alagic, 2004).

Cage Painting Learning Environment

Learning Processes

The CPLE embodies two learning cycles (Figure 2.10) that may be considered as embedded in a cognitive apprenticeship within a situated learning paradigm (e.g., Collins, Brown, & Newman, 1989). The first learning cycle (simulations-based), depicted as the upper small circle in Figure 2.10, refers to the learner being guided through specific cognitive and metacognitive strategies as he or she plays some simulations. The second learning cycle, CPLE-based (shown in the lower, larger circle), comprises engaging the learner by stimulating his/her curiosity about prior experience of a cultural misunderstanding that is caused by a *preconception* or a more extreme *disorienting dilemma* and then prompting him/her to reflect on this experience. After reflecting, the learner plays a number of simulations which constitute a form of concrete experience, and then derives some strategies that can be applied to future intercultural encounters, real or virtual (the first learning process). The learner can participate in the active experimentation aspect by designing his/her own scenario, thus completing the second process. Within the two learning processes, CPLE provides a structure for closing the learning process loops through: reflective observation, concrete experiences in a virtual environment, abstract conceptualization of CP strategies and an active

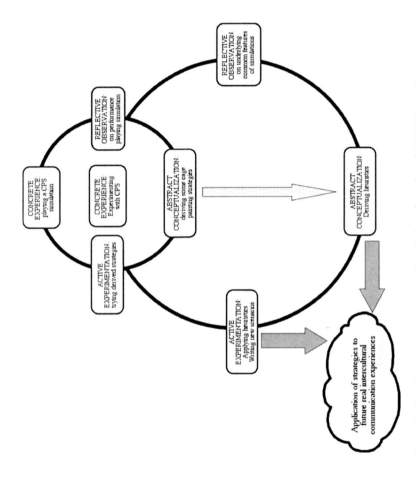

Figure 2.10. Learning processes: Simulations-based and CPLE-based learning cycles.

experimentation stage through designing new scenarios, (e.g., Kolb, 1984; Kolb & Fry, 1975). Prompting learners to reflect on prior, real-life experiences of preconceptions or disorienting dilemmas associated with communication stimulates *engagement*. Gaining concrete experience corresponds to *exploration* and abstract conceptualization is in effect a process of *explanation*. That leads to experimentation in which the ICC heuristic is applied in new scenarios as a form of *elaboration*. As the learner progresses to the second learning process, the explanation and experimentation activities lead to the writing of new scenarios. As other learners play new simulations arising from these scenarios, the author can *evaluate* the effectiveness of his/her scenarios as learning tools for developing ICC competence, thus completing the learning process (e.g., Karplus & Thier, 1967; Yeotis, Alagic, & Gibson, 2004).

Interface

The CP Simulator interface (Figure 2.7) mimics an interactive chat session as depicted in the window on the left-hand side of the interface. The difference is that instead of entering text, the learner chooses from a list of five choices at each step from the text bubble on the right-hand side of the interface. The character in the foreground at the bottom of the interface represents the learner and the other character represents Simea. Part of the way through a simulation, each character is surrounded by a partly painted/shaded cage as a result of the combinations of choices made by the learner. In the chat window there are icons attached to each paragraph that correspond to Simea and the learner. Each time the learner selects a choice and presses the *Send* button; their contribution is added to the chat window, followed by Simea's reaction. At the same time, the Hint window at the bottom of the chat window offers some feedback and advice and the cage bars are updated.

Online Scenario Repository

An online CPLE scenario repository has been established (http://gl.wichita.edu/CPS/). It allows users to play existing simulations (Figure 2.7) and write new scenarios, using a template (Figures 2.9a-f). When the learner judges that the scenario is complete, he/she can generate a simulation, based on that scenario. It can be further revised after testing and can become part of the generally available CP simulations in the online repository of the CPLE. For example, a class of graduate students, who are school teachers, can work in teams of three or four to write a scenario that deals with an intercultural misunderstanding of their choice. The scenarios written by the teams can be added to the online scenario repository and made available for other learners.

Scenarios can also be written to help K-12 students to prepare for embarking on intercultural exchange activities, both direct (face-to-face) and/or communication technology mediated.

Scenarios as Learning Objects

The CPLE with its online scenario repository is a Web 2.0 based situated learning environment that can assist in facilitating learner-driven experiences and promote cognitive processing. Brenda Bannan-Ritland, Nada Dabbagh, and Kate Murphy (2002) refer to this type of learning environment as a *learning object system*. Cage painting scenarios are modular in nature, which means that they can be selected and combined for different emphases and contexts (Bannan-Ritland et al., 2002; Wiley, 2000). Thus, scenarios are *learning objects*. The CPLE scenario repository is supported with *metadata*, or descriptors used to identify and characterize scenarios such as the topic of a scenario. A critical factor in the authoring of scenarios is the context. This is one of the elements of a scenario, which improves its utility as a learning object. A weakness of many learning objects is their lack of adaptability for new contexts (Lemire, 2006), which in the case of the CPLE takes on a different meaning. It is expected that the number and variety of scenarios as well as their modular nature will provide many opportunities for the development of learners' context-sensitive ICC strategies. Clearly, this interpretation of *new contexts* is different from the one that Lemire had in mind, but from an educational point of view, it justifies consideration of the CPLE as a dynamic learning object system (Alagic, Gibson, & Rimmington, 2007).

Clusters of Simulation Scenarios

Each CP scenario is designed to be sufficient to allow the learner to resolve an intercultural misunderstanding that is precipitated by a preconception or disorienting dilemma and to practice the four cage painting strategies (Figure 2.5). The structure of the scenario (Figure 2.8) is not too complex for an author or a team of authors to create a new scenario in a reasonable amount of time, using the associated template (Figures 2.9a-f). The goal, context and nature of the intercultural misunderstanding can be made increasingly complex. For example, early scenarios may present situations in which Simea is an equal in power to the learner (e.g., peers), while later scenarios can present instances where Simea has a different power status, lower or higher, than the learner. However, there is a limit to the level of complexity that can be included in just one scenario. The modular nature of scenarios makes it possible to handle more complex and interrelated intercultural misunderstandings in clusters of scenarios as depicted in Figure 2.11 for *Education* or *Business*. For example,

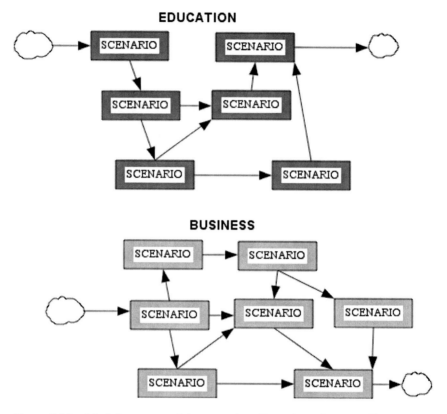

Figure 2.11.   Modular nature of the scenarios allows clustering according to various themes.

the Education cluster may be concerned with a number of interrelated issues in a diverse classroom, such as body language, learning styles and colloquialisms in a second language. The Business cluster may contain scenarios on different parts of an ongoing negotiation between enterprises located in different countries.

Data Generation and Analysis

While playing a simulation, if the learner has made a good choice, he/she receives appropriate feedback and the cage bars become darker (Figure 2.7). If the learner made a mediocre choice, it usually means only one cage was painted and so the bars of one or the other cage will become darker, plus the learner receives the feedback. If the learner made a bad choice there is no change to the cages and he/she receives feedback to help him/her make a better choice in the next step. After four steps, if the

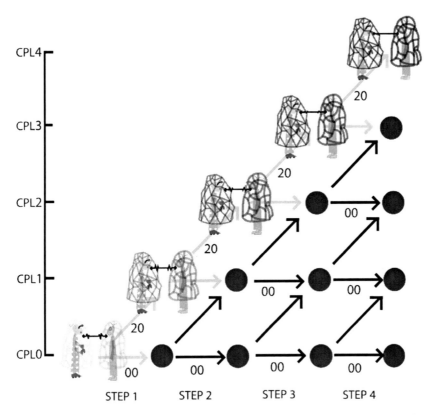

Figure 2.12.   CP simulation trajectory matrix: Strings of numbers represent the learner's performance.

learner has made four good choices, the cage bars will be black. However, if the learner has made four bad choices, the bars remain invisible (Figure 2.12). Usually, with the amount of scaffolding (Simea's responses, hints, and cage bars) even for the first simulation, the learner will make some mediocre or good choices.

As the learner plays a simulation within the CPLE, it generates a record of his/her performance. When the learner makes a good choice, a score of 20 is recorded, when the learner makes a mediocre choice, a score of 10 is recorded and when the learner makes a bad choice, a score of 00 is recorded. Each simulation generates a string of numbers that represent the learner's performance for each of the four steps, (e.g., 00 10 20 10). In this manner, the learner follows a trajectory through a matrix of combinations of CPLs (CPL0 to CPL4) reached after each of steps 1 to 4 (Figure 2.12). As the learner selects Good choices, he/she receives a score of 20 and proceeds to the next level with the cages becoming more opaque and the interference with messages, represented as squiggles in the arrows, becoming diminished. On the other extreme, selection of Bad choices results in no change to CPL and a score of 00. During a simulation the learner may follow a trajectory somewhere between the two extremes.

To increase the benefit to the learner of using the CPLE for improving their ICC, and to facilitate the learner's metacognitive thinking, it is beneficial to accompany the simulations with a process of guided reflective journaling. Before playing a simulation for the first time, it is helpful to have a learner reflect on an incident, a miscommunication or incorrect contextualization from their own experience. In some cases, such an instance may have remained unresolved. In others, the learner may have explored the basis of the incident in terms of his/her own perspective and that of the other person and then he/she may have overcome that incident. Triggering reflection about such intercultural misunderstandings creates a connection of prior experiences with the CPLE context. After playing one or a few CP simulations, it is useful to share and reflect with others on his/her performance and what strategies may have emerged as being useful. After a period of time, when the learner has played a number of scenarios or themed clusters (Figure 2.11), reflecting on the contribution to real-life situations of the cage painting strategies he/she has learned, (Hartman, Moskal, & Dziuban, 2006) may narrow the transfer distance to the potential target context (Figure 2.3). The CPLE facilitates connection between knowing and doing by providing these ongoing opportunities for learners to experiment with different clusters and to develop their own scenarios.

The type of guided reflection questions to pose for learners will depend on the context, the learners and the topic or content framework, within which ICC development is being integrated. Questions for senior engineering design students working in globally distributed, multicultural teams may be inappropriate for junior high school students collaborating on a foreign language/geography project with counterparts in another country. These two groups would have significant differences in their age, backgrounds, interests, and life experiences.

Together, the quantitative performance data and qualitative, guided reflective journal entries are used for multiple purposes. Analysis of the performance data indicates learning trends for sequences of particular simulations (Rimmington, Gibson, & Alagic, 2007). Certain scenarios or types of scenarios are not effective in a particular context. For example, graduate students in education can better relate to scenarios from classroom situations than from engineering design laboratories or corporate boardrooms. Such quantitative analysis may identify "faulty" scenarios that need refinement. Sets of guided reflective questions applied

Table 2.1. Sample Prompts for Guided Reflection on CPLE

Sample Prompts for Guided Cognitive/Metacognitive Reflection	*Purpose*
What is your ethnic/cultural heritage?	Research-Demographic
Describe a situation in which you said something to another person that was misunderstood and what you did to rectify the situation. You can also use an example from someone that you know or from the literature/media.	Cognitive—linking to prior concrete experience
What learning strategies are emerging from playing some CP simulations that you will apply in subsequent simulations or in real life?	Metacognitive—abstract conceptualization
How can the CPLE be improved?	Formative evaluation
Did you learn enough about Simea's perspective in steps 1 and 2 to be successful in steps 3 and 4?	Research-improvement

at different times in relation to CP simulations can be constructed to allow: (a) assessment of the learners' progress (cognitive and metacognitive), (b) diagnosis of learning difficulties or problems with a scenario, (c) formative evaluation, or (d) inquiry about learners' conceptualization of the ICC (e.g., Table 2.1 above).

Cage Painting Laws

Inspired by Frampton F. Fox's (2003) seven laws for *virtual culture training*, we contextualized a similar set of nine laws for cage painting, namely: dialectic thinking, the iceberg effect, listening, emotive experience, reflexivity, ICC heuristic, complementarity, variety, pilgrimage, and experience-knowledge tension.

Dialectic thinking. Cage painting involves dialectic thinking as the interactants seek a common ground. This process is aided by an understanding and application of the ICC dialectics (Martin & Nakayama, 1999) that are described in more detail in chapter 1. An important point of reference in the foreground of dialectic thinking is the power relationship between interactants. The "Privilege-Disadvantage" dialectic (Figure 1.4) is an instance of potential power distance between interactants. As people of different cultures learn more about each other, the ongoing process of cage painting may involve consideration of many different intercultural dialectics.

Iceberg effect. Misunderstandings around which scenarios are designed can be of varying levels of complexity depending on how deeply particular beliefs are held. To achieve resolution of deeper intercultural conflicts related to traditions, beliefs and values in the *iceberg* metaphor (Ting-Toomey & Chung, 2005) will require resolution through one or more scenarios. Just as some parts of the iceberg are deeper than others, some cage bars may be "deeper" or more difficult to paint. The iceberg effect will affect the required length of the cage painting process needed to achieve resolution.

Listening. The CP simulations will most likely lose value if time is not allowed for the learner to consider choices (e.g., wait time, considering alternative interpretations) as he/she plays a scenario and then reflects on his/her progress within a scenario as well as for developing the cage painting strategies after a number of scenarios. The learner needs the time to (a) gain experience from the scenarios, (b) reflect on the experience, (c) derive the cage painting strategies through abstract conceptualization, and (d) apply them in subsequent scenarios. Depending on the learner, it may take playing a few or many scenarios to develop a deep understanding of the ICC heuristic. Along the way, while playing simulations or designing scenarios, the learner may also achieve an understanding of holding multiple perspectives (Ishii, 1984; Rimmington, Gruba, Gordon, Gibson, & Gibson, 2004).

Emotive experience. ICC is an activity that requires mindfulness (Langer, 1989; Nagata, 2007) and reflection-in-action (Schön, 1983). Triggering emotions to which the learner can relate enhances the learning experience and the level of transfer. Therefore, as CP scenarios are designed, it is important to consider the emotional dimension of the cultural misunderstanding being simulated (e.g., Looking into my eyes, Figures 2.9a-f). This can be enhanced with attention to the language used in the scripts of the learner and Simea. Anger and curt choices in response to displeasing situations with no sensitivity to Simea may be chosen when these emotions are triggered in the learner. The learner will discover that such choices do not contribute positively to the situation. This underlines the need for careful metacognitive scaffolding through guided reflections.

Reflexivity. Embedding the CP simulations within guided reflective journaling (Schön, 1987) will stimulate metacognitive thinking and increase the value of the simulations. Careful choice of guiding questions (National Research Council, 2000) can help the learner relate to prior experiences of intercultural misunderstandings. They can bring the learner's focus onto the cage painting strategies and how they might be used in real-life intercultural interactions.

ICC heuristic. When involved in an especially challenging intercultural interaction, resorting to the cage painting questioning strategies may help move out of an impasse. During initial socialization, repeating CPL1 and CPL2 allows interactants to develop a comfortable conversational atmosphere and acquire the knowledge needed to advance to CPL3 and CPL4 (Figure 2.5).

Complementarity. Adding other learning materials and strategies can enhance the effectiveness of the CPLE. For example, using the CPLE as a resource within an ICC course along with role-plays and examples of intercultural literature will complement each other's value. Some examples of relevant intercultural literature include *On Being Foreign* (Lewis & Jungman, 1986), *The Art of Crossing Cultures* (Storti, 1990) and *Letters Back to Ancient China* (Rosendorfer, 1997).

Variety. As more authors with different cultural perspectives contribute scenarios in different languages, the CPLE will increase the variety of examples needed to prepare learners for the many situations that await them. A substantial collection of scenarios will help learners to appreciate the complexity of ICC, as it exists in the many combinations and permutations of cultures, languages and contexts.

Pilgrimage. One advantage of CPLE simulations is that they encourage learners to become "tuned in" to cultural characteristics and their effects on their cultural proficiency level (Lindsey, Robins, & Terrell, 2003) and ICCC (e.g., Gudykunst, 1998). As preparation for lifelong learning, the intent is that CPLE and application of CP strategies piques the learner's curiosity to seek new intercultural opportunities. To achieve success in ICC,

> one must transcend one's own system... What is more, the only way to master either is to seek out systems that are different to one's own.... The rules governing behaviour and structure of one's own cultural system can be discovered only in a specific context or real-life situation. (Hall, 1977, p. 51)

Experience-knowledge tension. Contemporary learning theories emphasize that the learning cycle approach produces the best learning result if it starts with an experience (Kolb, 1984; Lawson, Abraham, & Renner, 1989), and that the learning cycle approach can stimulate self-regulated learning (Yeotis et al., 2004). CP simulations are designed to provide discovery-type experiences. Although virtual, these experiences, when followed by reflection, will provide conditions for a successful transfer to real-life situations (Perkins & Salomon, 1992). Cage painting simulations are not a substitute for real experiences, but they can accelerate the process of developing cage painting strategies and hence be of value during intercultural interactions.

SUMMARY: WHERE WE ARE AND WHERE WE ARE GOING?

In chapter 1 we discussed the global and ICC competences. This began with an examination of culture and cultural metaphors, leading to the cage metaphor. Then we turned our attention to the role of dialectic thinking in ICC. From this emerged the notion of cage painting, which happens as a third place process. The cage painting metaphor is a helpful conceptual tool for understanding ICC. In this chapter 2, we described a tool derived from the cage painting metaphor—the CPLE. The CPLE has two learning processes: an inner cycle associated with playing simulations and an outer cycle in which learners advance to scenario authoring. An example of a scenario is presented to illustrate the ICC heuristic with its four questioning strategies. We conclude with the cage painting laws. In the chapter 3 next we will explore the philosophical and theoretical underpinnings of this approach to ICC, the integration of an intercultural dialectic and conclude with conditions and catalysts for facilitating third place processes (Figure 2.13).

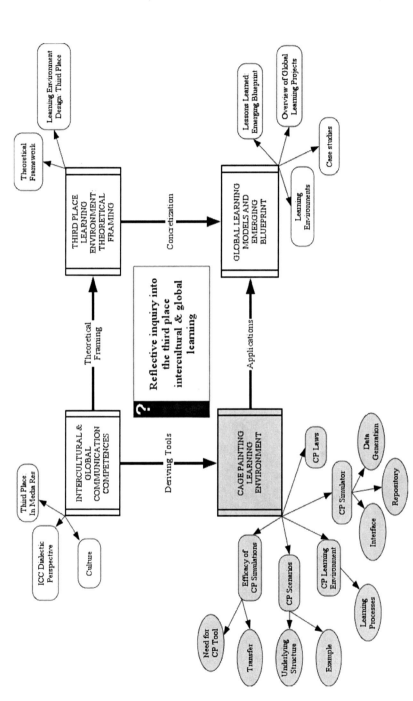

Figure 2.13. Searching for a conceptual tool for developing ICC and GCC.

CHAPTER 3

THIRD PLACE PROCESSES

Theoretical Framing

INTRODUCTION

In this chapter, first, we present a theoretical framework within which the ideas of chapters 1 and 2 are grounded. Second, we set the stage for the global learning models and an emerging instructional design about which we deliberate in chapter 4. Chapter 1 focused on *intercultural and global communication competences*, framed by culture and communication relative to environment and power relationships. We contend that dialectic thinking is essential for development of these competences. Two main points of chapter 1 are, first, the use of the cage painting metaphor to represent dialogic coconstruction of meaning, and second, the recognition of the need to facilitate third place processes in intercultural or global settings. Chapter 2 was about the *cage painting learning environment*, an online learning system, which contains a simulation-based tool for improving intercultural communication (ICC) strategies. The tool is derived from the cage painting metaphor and it serves to prepare learners for intercultural interactions in both global and local, culturally diverse contexts.

The theoretical framework components that are supporting ideas from Chapters 1 and 2 are grounded in the philosophies of critical social theory, social constructivism, and dialectic thinking. Furthermore, they are

Third Place Learning: Reflective Inquiry Into Intercultural and Global Cage Painting
pp. 69–107
Copyright © 2008 by Information Age Publishing

providing an appropriate conjectural background for reporting about global learning models (chapter 4, this volume) and an emerging instructional design blueprint for intercultural learning environments that model and facilitate *Third Place Processes.*

THEORETICAL FRAMEWORK

Intercultural and global communication competences (chapter 1, this volume) and an online learning system design that uses the conceptual tool, *cage painting,* (chapter 2, this volume) are framed by a theoretical bricolage. This bricolage, emerging from a combination of the philosophy of critical social theory and social constructivist learning, has the following underlying components: critical multiculturalism and pedagogy within *critical social theory* (Freire, 1968/1970; Kincheloe, 2005; Kincheloe & Steinberg, 1997; Shor, 2002); transformative learning (Mezirow, 1991; Taylor, 1997); and within *social constructivist learning theories*: situated cognition (Brown, Collins, & Duguid, 1989), cultural dialectic (Martin & Nakayama, 1999) and reflective action (Langer, 1989; Nagata, 2006; Schön, 1983).

Underlying Philosophy

Critical social theory, according to Michael Crotty (2003), set the stage for diversified ideas, as opposed to a single perspective approach for interpreting the world. This theory is based on: (a) acknowledgment that traditional theory merely describes a situation, while critical thinking seeks change to achieve social justice; (b) knowledge that critical thinking focuses on self-emancipation and social change; (c) radical examination of underlying social relationships in society that involve dominance and subordination in given situations; (d) exploration of the link between societal power structures and the influences on everyday life, including education; and (e) belief that awareness is power (Giroux, 2003; Kincheloe, 2005). Furthermore, critical social theory typically refers to traditions that originate from the Frankfurt school of critical theory, which arose in the 1940s at the Institute of Social Research within the University of Frankfurt, Germany. There, philosophies emanated from the seminal works of Georg Wilhelm Friedrich Hegel, Karl Marx, Immanuel Kant, and Max Weber. These philosophies critiqued the existing power structure in society and articulated the quest for human freedom and societal democracies. Critical Social Theory also gave rise to the twentieth century emancipatory political movements such as race and feminist theory and politics of difference (Crotty, 2003; Kincheloe, 2005; Wink, 2005). Emerging from critical social theory is critical pedagogy.

Critical Pedagogy

Critical pedagogy arose from the work of Brazilian critical educator Paulo Freire (1968/1970). Critical pedagogy seeks to reenergize teachers and inspire students to make a difference and to push education into new qualitative domains. This theory involves a vision of transforming power relationships. It allows the learner to become aware of the power relationships in which they are embedded, thereby allowing them to effect changes that will redress the power imbalance. The perpetuation of existing unbalanced power structures through the education system is called *reproduction,* drawing on Marx's notion of the reproduction of power relations through social and economic structures. Freire believed that learning places can be oppressive for many students by silencing their voices and experiences, thus maintaining the sociopolitical status quo. An example of this form of oppression is the use of an unchanging dominant host culture lens during intercultural interactions, both local and global. This constitutes an obstacle to an understanding of multiple perspectives. Therefore, critical thinking, especially critical self-awareness, is an essential element of intercultural learning (Chen, 1989). Effective learning will cultivate critical conscience—Freire's *conscientization* of learners—to achieve in-depth understanding of both self and the world. He utilized the concept of conscientization in a similar manner to the way Ellen Langer (1989) used the concept of *mindfulness*, or Adair Linn Nagata (2003) employed the concept of *bodymindfulness*, although in a different context. An important part of conscientized learning is active dialog, which requires mutual respect and a willingness to collaborate. As learners form their understanding of others and themselves, they are collectively interpreting and changing the world. In turn, participants of this changed world act as agents of mediation on future dialogs among intercultural learners (Freire, 1968/1970; Kincheloe, 2005; Shor, 2002; Wink, 2005).

Critical pedagogy, as an element of learning, involves collaborative problem-solving, critical conversations, and the explicit inclusion of the various perspectives of diverse participants. It shares much in common with the philosophies of John Dewey's (1910/1933) and Paulo Freire's (1968/1970) premises that learning goals should be based on the learner's history, experiences, and culture. This pedagogical approach em ' ------
the inclusion of all voices, which is an important condition for fos
third place processes. Real dialogue that demands critical
reflection, discussion, and negotiation, will afford the necessary c

for everyone to reach beyond their own cultural boundaries (Kincheloe, 2005) into the Homi K. Bhabha's (1994) Third Space. Critical pedagogy involves reviewing our perspective and rewriting our world. Facilitators of intercultural learning must come to understand that critical pedagogy is about learning, relearning, and even unlearning (Wink, 2005). Unlearning is very different from relearning, because it may be quite uncomfortable. To use an analogy, relearning can be likened to the challenge of moving to another state and getting a new driver's license. The challenge will include learning some new rules and then remembering them as you undergo your driver's test and begin driving. Unlearning will occur when moving to another country, where the cars are driven on the other side of the road. It is not just a matter of learning some new rules. You have to deal with a different perspective. Many behaviors that have become second nature, no longer apply, for example looking to the left or right for oncoming traffic. This is a matter of life and death! You have to put these habits out of your mind (unlearning) and learn to cope with driving on the other side of the road (relearning). Continuing with the analogy, the learner has to be mindful of being on a different side of the road and let go of any attachment he or she has to rules or habits associated with being on the *other* side of the road before he or she can move on.

Critical Multiculturalism

Multiculturalism has been understood and defined in various ways, ranging from simple recognition of cultural and ethnic diversity to more critical identification of underlying power relationships. Bhikhu C. Parekh (2000) argued that it is not sufficient just to acknowledge a collection of different cultures, but rather that there is an extra ingredient. This ingredient is an explicit or conscious provision of the opportunity for interactions within which members of different cultures can share, negotiate, and enrich each other's culture. In this manner, Parekh provided a definition of multiculturalism that goes beyond the superficiality of being a façade that allows a dominant group to maintain the status quo. *Critical multiculturalism* provides a framework and pedagogical strategies to critique and challenge the prevailing cultural norms of a dominant group. Henry A. Giroux (1995) identified five elements of critical multiculturalism that we contend may inform third place learning processes:

— honoring cultural differences,
— comprehending *grand narratives*,
— understanding the relationship between difference and unity,

— uncovering the dynamics of power, and

— developing *border crossing* behavior.

The first essential element, *honoring cultural differences*, is the focus of discourse in which multiculturalism and equality become mutually reinforcing factors. Multicultural equality means that education in a world society should reflect the richness, color, and diversity of all its constituent cultural groups and individuals. It appears that one's context-dependent positions on the cultural proficiency continuum (Figure 1.10.), defined by Lindsey, Robins, and Terrell (2003), can affect significantly one's understanding and acceptance of multicultural equality and furthermore one's willingness to cross cultural boundaries and participate in third place (transformative) processes.

A second element of critical multiculturalism is about having the ability to analyze the texts and media about the "*grand narrative[s]*" (Mishra, 2005, p. 2) of the dominant culture. Such narratives contain vocabularies, which subtly promote stereotypes that ignore the history, culture, and identity of certain oppressed groups. The application of this second element implies mindfully analyzing not just the stereotypes and all other forms of discrimination, but how they are produced and perpetuated. The concept of grand narrative has similarities with Michel Foucault's (1980) idea of discourse.

The third element establishes a *relationship between difference and unity* so as to prevent deterioration into binarism. Binarism operates in such a way that the center expels its undesirable traits, creating an antithetical identity, the *other*, that is projected outside the center (Rutherford, 1990; Young, 1990). In dichotomous thinking, these undesirable *others* are labeled as whatever we exclude from our positive self-valuation. In contemporary Western contexts, such other identities include *terrorist, communist* or *Islamist*." In order to avoid binarism, it is important to carefully consider a unity-in-difference position in which all voices are heard. It is neither a melting pot of assimilation, nor a cultural hierarchy. It is a *celebrationist* dialogical and dialectic process within, "a borderland, a site of crossing, negotiation, translation and dialogue" (Mishra, 2005, p. 121), or third place processes in which diverse voices are heard (Bhabha, 1994).

Power structure comprises interplay of formal institutional and informal practices that result in inequities. More importantly, power differences reach into the education systems, which then perpetuate or even magnify these differences. Giroux's (1995) fourth element is about the need to go beyond merely acknowledging cultural differences toward gaining an understanding of how inequities relate to the power structure of a world society. Incorporating critical multiculturalism into intercultural learning, both global and local, can draw attention to *uncovering the dynamics of power*

bullying

that result in domination, oppression (Freire, 1968/1970) and even humiliation (Lindner, 2006a; Lindner, 2006b) throughout world societies.

Critical multiculturalism, according to Henry Giroux's (1995) fifth element, cannot be imposed or derived in a transmission or banking model of learning that assumes teacher's authority and student's uncritical learning. Instead, it emerges in a constructivist-learning environment that encourages active and open dialog between all stakeholders in the community. Educators or leaders need to model *border crossing* (Giroux, 1992) behavior as they lead learners through an apprenticeship of critical multiculturalism. In addition to modeling, the educators need to be able to create conditions for candid and open dialog and power-cognizant inquiry for (intercultural) learning.

Critical multiculturalism engages in and honors diversity; it promotes an analysis that is mindful and avoids stereotyping and dichotomy. It holds a unity-in-difference position and uncovers the dynamics of power. Consistent with intercultural learning and cultural competency, critical multiculturalism cannot be imposed, but needs to be modeled in a supportive and affirming learning environment.

Another model one might draw on to ground the approach taken here is that of James A. Banks' (2006) dimensions of the critical multiculturalism. It includes *content integration* along with knowledge construction, equity pedagogy, prejudice reduction, and empowerment of school culture and social structure. While this framework was developed from an American perspective and focuses on internal racial/ethnic relations, it shares some features with Henry Giroux's (1995) elements of critical multiculturalism and may be applied, with some modification to intercultural/global learning. For example, integration of global interactions into courses in different content areas involves facilitating dialog and reflection to interweave elements of culture and content. This is similar to what Banks called "content integration" (p. 133). Banks' description of "knowledge construction" (p. 133) falls within the broader framework of the social constructivist approach. The latter emphasizes dialogic coconstruction of meaning and identity (Rimmington, Gibson, & Alagic, 2007). By providing opportunities for direct interaction with members of another culture, intercultural interaction helps to overcome preconceptions associated with prejudice and stereotyping as well as giving all participants a voice. In a broader sense this discourages the creation or perpetuation of other people as *objects*. The goal for students participating in global/local intercultural learning is to experience a shift in power away from the teacher and an equalization of power between their respective cultures with the focus being on their interactions.

From the foregoing, it can be seen that critical multicultural theory takes a prominent place in our theoretical framing of ICC competence and cage painting. The humanistic concept of critical multiculturalism is based upon values of proactive commitment to foster cultural pluralism (Grant & Ladson-Billings, 1997), diversity, human rights, and social justice for all people, an approach to teaching and learning that builds understanding about ethnic groups and cultures. A fundamental view of critical multiculturalism is the need for our experiences to be seen from different perspectives, which then encourages and supports perspective taking (Banks, 1996; Bennett, 1990; Bennett, 1993; Nieto, 1999, 2004).

Perspective taking challenges the view that knowledge is objective and exposes learners to the idea that knowledge is socially constructed. Through critical thinking, dialog and taking the perspective of another person, knowledge is deconstructed and reconstructed to critically include diverse points of view. This contributes to the development of a qualitatively new perspective that is more inclusive and continuously and critically examined. Although changes in pedagogy and affirming students' diversity may be helpful, without a critical perspective, multicultural education can be superficial (Kincheloe & Steinberg, 1997; Nieto, 1999). After considering critical social theory, critical pedagogy, and critical multiculturalism as important elements of intercultural learning, we now turn our attention to a suitable learner-centered educational theory.

LEARNING THEORY

The contemporary science of learning identifies learning as a multidisciplinary endeavor. It explores multiple perspectives and insights into mental functioning as well as into the cultural and social context of learning (National Research Council, 2000). Emerging from these general assumptions is our theoretical framing of intercultural learning, which centers on the dialectical and dynamic nature of learning; learning as a set of dialogical processes, and the critical place of the learning context. The learning theory considered here incorporates aspects of situated cognition, transformative learning, and reflective action or reflection-in-action. Two expected outcomes are the development of consciousness of the other person's perspectives and an improved understanding of one's own perspective. Learners construct these perspectives through dialog and consideration of alternative views (Bednar, Cunningham, Duffy, & Perry, 1992; Tam, 2000).

As asserted above, a person's knowing or meaning making is founded in his/her beliefs and experiences. The fundamental assumption is that people construct new knowledge and understandings for themselves based on beliefs, experiences, and prior knowledge (e.g., Cobb, Piaget, 1977; Piaget & Inhelder, 1967; Tudge & Winterhoff, vygotsky, 1978). According to Terry L. Simpson (2002), this is an episte-mology, a philosophical explanation regarding the nature of learning that is often named a constructivist learning theory. Among different types of constructivist learning theories, *social constructivism* focuses on dialogic meaning making resulting from interactions between individuals and their environment. The differences among constructivist theories are based on the particular role given to social interactions when constructing knowledge. Epistemological theories range from the notion that mental structures exactly reflect reality to the view that the individual's mental world is the only reality. Within this theoretical framework, it is assumed that knowledge is partly objective and partly socially constructed. That is to say, it lies within the continuum of constructivist epistemologies. Many authors emphasize the influence of the social environment on learning. Albert Bandura's (1986) social cognitive theory, and Jerome Seymour Bruner's (1984, 1990) and Lev Semenovich Vygotsky's (1978, 1981) developmental theories held that knowledge derives from interactions between individuals and their environments (*social constructivism*). Our approach to intercultural learning is positioned within the domains of social constructivism and cognitive learning theory. This position is paral-lel to being between a belief in the existence of an independent world (objectivist ontology) and a belief that the world is just a series of percep-tions and meanings (subjectivist ontology). It is important to mention here some of the major points of Vygotsky's (1978) theories summarized by Dale H. Schunk (2004):

- Knowledge is coconstructed through social interactions;
- Internal representations are developed that support self-regula-tion;
- Language is developed, from social to private and to inner dialog; and
- Cultural exchange of language, symbols, and artifacts guides human development (selected and adapted items from Schunk, 2004, Table 7.2, p. 295).

The following sections on situated cognition, transformative learning, and reflective action capture the essential aspects of theories that support our conceptualization of third place learning processes. The interplay between these learning theories and the underlying philosophy, described in the previous section, establishes the theoretical foundation of our learning theory that can be transformative in its nature and can be applied in both global and local contexts.

Situated Cognition

A fundamental assumption of social constructivism is that cognitive processes, thinking and learning included, are situated in social and environmental contexts (Greeno, 1989). Situated cognition entails the intuitive notion that learning is the result of the interaction of many processes; situated cognition is pertinent to how learning occurs. The same applies to intercultural learning, keeping in mind that global-reach-based interactions are becoming more commonplace, thanks to global interconnectedness. Furthermore, research points to the relevance of exploring situated cognition as a means of understanding the development of competence in various domains (Cobb, 1994; Lampert, 1990). In this book we are focusing on intercultural and global competences as they apply to both global and culturally diverse local contexts.

Central to the perspective of situated cognition is the view that knowing is either contextualized or abstracted from different experiences. Knowing may be viewed as "functional stance on the interaction, not a 'truth' " (Barab & Duffy, 2000, p. 3); it is coconstructed in the individual-environment interaction. Many authors emphasize the reciprocal nature of interactions in which cognition and meaning are socially and culturally coconstructed (e.g., Lave & Wenger, 1991; Palencia, 1998). The way in which knowledge is used to solve a problem will be determined by the culture and the context that encompasses an activity. In a significant way, learning can be described as a process of enculturation (Brown et al., 1989). Therefore, situated learning occurs when students work on authentic tasks that take place in a real-world setting (Winn, 1993). Knowing is situated, resulting from activity, context, and culture in which it is developed and to be used. This implies that learning strategies embedded in authentic situations are essential for meaningful learning; meaningful learning will take place if it is embedded in the social and physical context within which it will be used (Brown et al., 1989; Hannafin, Land, & Oliver, 1999).

Cognitive Apprenticeship

Within the situated learning paradigm, intercultural learning may be structured as a cognitive apprenticeship. Cognitive apprenticeship is an instructional model within the situated learning paradigm where learners participate in a sequence of guided activities and interact in ways similar to that of the craft apprentice. It differs from craft apprenticeship because of its emphasis on the development of cognitive and metacognitive strategies. Cognitive apprenticeship suggests authentic tasks for learners and appropriate scaffolding by the teacher. Students' tasks are authentic and more substantive than they can manage independently, but only so tha they require the aid of peers' and instructors' scaffolding guidance. Knowledge and strategies are made meaningful by the context in which they are acquired. Modeling, coaching, fading, articulation, reflection, and exploration of ideas are the most significant phases of this learning process. A well-structured and facilitated cognitive apprenticeship develops not only the cognitive strategies, but also the metacognitive ones required for true expertise (Alagic, Yeotis, Rimmington, & Koert, 2003). Learning activities using the cognitive apprenticeship method should include the following key characteristics:

(a) Introductory tasks should be based in familiar activities that allow the students to build upon their prior and tacit knowledge,
(b) The problem should provide for a variety of heuristic approaches, and
(c) Only after the process becomes meaningful to learners, the appropriate heuristics used by practitioners may be introduced (Brown et al., 1989).

In addition to modeling of processes by experts, cognitive apprenticeship structure (Herrington & Oliver, 1995) needs to include the following provisions:

- an authentic, culturally diverse context;
- substantive activities, authentic to the given discipline area;
- consideration of multiple roles and perspectives;
- collaborative, dialogic coconstruction of knowledge;
- coaching and scaffolding at critical times (e.g., disorienting dilemma);
- metacognitive and critical reflection to enable *abstractions* to be formed;
- articulation and inquiry to enable tacit knowledge to be made explicit; and
- integrated assessment of learning within the tasks.

For example, this can be accomplished by establishing teams of globally distributed members from different cultures, who are required to k together to achieve a goal that relates to their chosen career or to bject matter at hand. The learners' team work will be helped by riate modeling by instructors and the provision of guiding ques- t prompt critical reflection about the intercultural interactions implications for successful team work. This type of learning he discussed in more detail in later sections/chapters. Now we

turn our attention from underlying learning theories and
need for transformative learning for effective intercultur:

Transformative Learning and Dialectic Thinking

Within this emerging theoretical framework, learning is largely derived
from the social environment with recognition that culture significantly
affects knowledge construction (Schunk, 2004). An illustration of the
hazards inherent in the construction of new knowledge based on tacit "*assumed*"
knowledge that is derived from an individual's context is provided in a
story *Fish is Fish* (Lionni, 1970) and elaborated on in the National
Research Council (2000) book titled *How People Learn*. There are many *unspoken*
other examples that demonstrate how tacit knowledge can make it difficult to understand new information. This illustrates one of the major
challenges of learning: the *unlearning* of poorly constructed ideas that
cause misunderstandings while communicating with others. This is especially true for those ideas stemming from early development during
enculturation into the home culture. To understand the link between
transformative intercultural learning and the dialectic way of thinking, we
need to deconstruct the dialectic and consider its implications for critical
thinking, which we do in the following section.

Dialectic Thinking

The dialectic process of learning has in its essence questioning of fixed
propositions, perspectives or points of view (thesis). It requires considering not only its direct *opposite* but more broadly, *what thesis is not, what it*
omits or excludes (antithesis). The outcome might be neither thesis nor the
antithesis, but instead a qualitatively new proposition, a synthesis. The
synthesis in turn can become a new thesis, which leads to the dialectic spiral of *thesis-antithesis-synthesis-thesis* (TAS) (Figure 3.1). Although the TAS
sequence returns to a thesis, that thesis is different from the previous one.
Therefore the term dialectic *spiral* is more appropriate than *cycle*. This
brings about the realization that a position is as much defined by what it is
as by what it is not. *both/and not*

The process leading toward resolution of the incongruity between the *either/*
thesis and antithesis, and the dialogic coconstruction of meaning that *or.*
results in perspective consciousness, has its origins in the dialectics of
many cultures (Wong, 2006). The model with which we are most familiar
in the West has its roots in Ancient Greek philosophy, notably in the work
of Socrates and Plato, with later significant developments in the work of
Hegel, Marx, and Adorno. Thus, for example, Diogenes Laertius from
the third century A.D. offered the definition: "Dialectic is the art of

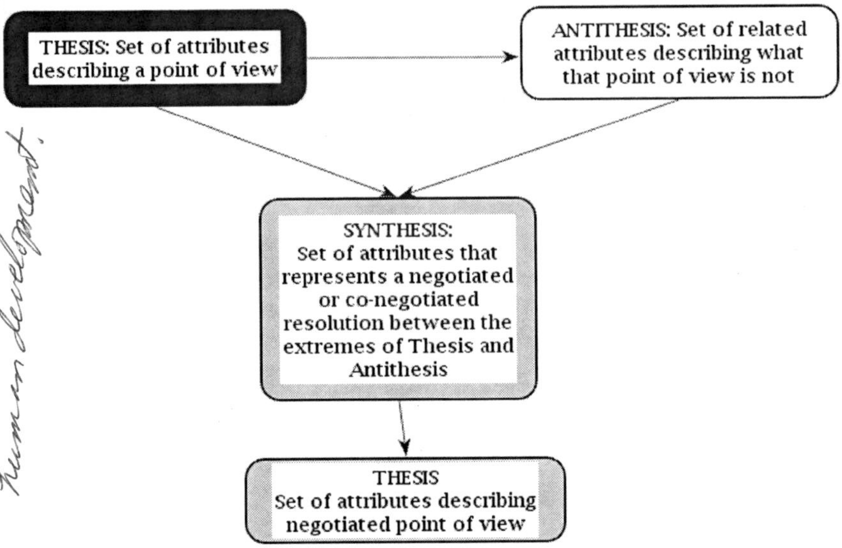

Figure 3.1.   A visualization of a dialectic step to a potential resolution of contra-dictory nature of thesis and antithesis.

discourse by which we either refute or establish some propositions by means of question and answer on the part of the interlocutors" (Laertius, 1925/ 2000, p. 319). It is also considered to be a transformation arising through substantive interactions where a dialectic perspective refers to a family of world-outlooks, which share three features—*change, wholeness,* and *internal relations* (Riegel, 1973). Dialectic thinking "reflects this orientation in the way in which it *engages in inquiry*" (Riegel, 1973, p. 24, authors' emphasis in italics). This type of thinking is characteristic of adult learning (Reason & Rowan, 1981) and challenges the individual to exercise the courage needed to move beyond the safety of intellectual security toward critical and open-minded reasoning. Within the dialectic perspective, phenomena that might otherwise be considered as obvious and fixed are viewed as transitory or in a constant state of *change*.

While this Platonic/Hegelian model is perhaps the most familiar, it is important to note that the TAS model is just one dialectic structure. Other examples from Wong (2006) include the *simple-changing-constant* concept from ancient Chinese culture, based on the ancient text *I Ching* (Book of Change) (Bhattacharya, 1977) and *perception-perceived-perceivor-negation-negated-negator* kernel of the ancient Indian negative dialectic (Madahyamika) (Basseches, 1984). After examining these other approaches to the dialectic, it can be concluded that the dialectic has existed for a long time in different cultures and that each culture has contributed some different interpretations about its process, form, and relationships.

What differentiates dialectic thinking from other approaches is its emphasis not only on change, but how change is driven through interaction of conflicting and opposing positions, rather than its being a smooth and continuous process. The relationship between thesis and antithesis can be conceptualized according to three themes: the *interdependence* of opposites, the *interpenetration* of opposites, and the *unity* of opposites (Reason & Rowan, 1981). The opposites depend on one another. Without dark, there is no light. In the region between the opposites there is transition or interpenetration. Metaphorically, at the extremes, there is unity of opposites. In the example of light and dark, at the dark extreme, there is blindness because light is needed to see and at the light extreme it is too bright to see, so again blindness exists.

Keriping Peng and Richard E. Nisbett (1999) use the yin-yang diagram (Figure 3.2) to illustrate how different parts determine each other (interdependence). Opposites can be found within each other (interpenetration) and the circle surrounding the parts represents their unity. In various shades of grey, which may represent a simplified view of syntheses in dialectic thinking, there is both some darkness and some lightness. A thesis-antithesis dichotomy presented above can be illustrated using a simple conceptualization of dialectic as a continuum between *opposites* represented as a line segment. Key examples would include: *logos* ↔ *ergon*

Figure 3.2.   The yin-yang symbol reflects relationships between the thesis and antithesis in a simplified, yet visually appealing form and shape.

(meaning ↔ action); individual ↔ collective; single perspective ↔ numerous perspectives; assimilation ↔ cultural pluralism; transmissive ↔ transformative; static ↔ dynamic; similarities ↔ differences; disadvantage ↔ privilege; history ↔ present; past ↔ future; subjective ↔ objective; ethnocentrism ↔ xenocentrism; autonomy ↔ connection; openness ↔ closedness.

For learners who have not been encouraged to think dialectically, who have come from the paradigm of fixed perspectives, the adoption of dialectic thinking constitutes an example of transformative learning. Without the elements of dialectic thinking described above, changes to point of view may be unlikely and changes to deeply held beliefs may be impossible. Fostering the practice of dialectic thinking in the context of intercultural learning is a prerequisite to learning that is transformative.

Transformative Learning

Within the framework of social constructivism, extended conceptualization of transformational learning includes attention to experience, critical reflection, dialectic thinking, and rational discourse of Jack Mezirow's (1991) theory (Taylor, 1997), with significant consideration given to psychoanalytic theory (Boyd & Myers, 1988). The literature on transformative learning theory reveals two somewhat contrasting approaches: *perspective transformation* associated with Mezirow's (e.g., 1991) work and *transformative education* (Boyd & Myers, 1988). Boyd and Myers base their work in analytical psychology, which focuses on *discernment* that leads to "contemplative insight, a personal illumination gained by putting things together and seeing them in their rational wholeness" (p. 274). This process is characterized by the following sequence:

(a) openness to alternative expressions of meaning,
(b) recognition of an essential connectedness between an incidentally triggered alternative perspective and the person's beliefs and behavior, and
(c) a disorienting dilemma, which is actually considered a "critical exercise of the discernment process" (p. 277).

Jack Mezirow (2000) used the terms meaning structure, frame of reference, habit of mind, and meaning perspective interchangeably to mean the structure of assumptions, perspectives, and expectations that act as a filter for our interpretation of the world. We will use the term *meaning structure*. The meaning structure is linked to individual's most guarded beliefs and deep—tacit knowledge based on learning that is assimilated without question during his/her formative years—enculturation. The individual has *points of view* that are predominantly shaped by his/her meaning structure along with adult learning experiences. Mezirow identified six overlapping aspects of meaning structure: sociolinguistic, moral-ethical, epistemic, philosophical, psychological, and aesthetic; which are selectively brought into the foreground depending on the context. In broad terms, there are two complex layers of meaning/knowledge: the point of view layer that is relatively easy to revise through learning, and the meaning structure layer that is very difficult to change through usual forms of learning. The point of view layer corresponds to the visible part of the iceberg, while the meaning layer corresponds to subsurface part of the iceberg (chapter 1, this volume). The latter requires the exposure or foregrounding of tacit or deeply ingrained knowledge and a critical mass of disorienting dilemmas or cognitive dissonance to trigger the change. This transformational change can be sudden due to immediate exposure to one significant, disorienting dilemma or incremental due to the gradual resolution of many smaller preconceptions or misconceptions; reconstruction of existing knowledge/concepts. In this context, Mezirow (2000) identifies four types of learning: transforming a point of view, refining of the meaning structure, transforming our meaning structure, and learning a new meaning structure. Each of these corresponds to the consideration of a thesis, one's current point of view or meaning structure, and an antithesis stemming from an alternative conception or disorienting dilemma. This dialectic consideration leads to a synthesis that corresponds to one of these four types of transformation.

The catalyst for the transformation of meaning structure is a *disorienting dilemma.* In the context of intercultural exchanges, an extreme disorienting dilemma (culture shock) may be encountering a custom of a host that is taboo in a visitor's culture, and at the same time, the acceptable equivalent in visitor's culture is taboo for the host, clearly a thesis and antithesis. Similar examples of extreme disorienting dilemmas include coping with becoming a paraplegic due to an accident, or losing your job for acting according to your moral values. Confronted with an intercultural challenge that has the magnitude of a disorienting dilemma, transformation of the meaning structure may require a single iteration through the dialectic spiral. Sometimes the transformation of an individual's meaning structure occurs as a cumulative effect of a critical number of transformations of points of view; many iterations along the dialectic spiral. Consider the person, who is learning to become an elementary school teacher but who suffers from mathematics anxiety due to their own negative school experiences. This notwithstanding, he or she will be required to teach mathematics. Teacher preparation programs create learning situations that result in small transformations of the learner's point of view ("I am not good at mathematics") that cumulatively lead to a transformation in self-concept or meaning structure ("I can understand some ideas in mathematics and I feel confident to teach mathematics"). It is important to realize that no single learning situation resulting from a preconception will necessarily result in a transformation of the meaning structure. It is either the critical mass of accumulated preconceptions that transform the point of view, or a single, more extreme disorienting dilemma that is needed to activate a transformation of the meaning structure.

In the case of the disorienting dilemma, an individual has no choice but to consider alternatives (thesis/antithesis). The car accident survivor who has paraplegia has to learn new ways to be mobile such as changing from sports such as cycling, to using a wheelchair. As he/she adapts, his/her outlook on life, or meaning structure, is changing as he/she moves along dialectic continua toward a new position of balance. Continuing this example, an observer may be able to *try on* the point of view of a person with paraplegia by pretending that his or her legs cannot be used for a day or a week. However, because the observer knows that he/she has the option of going back to the full use of his/her legs, he/she cannot actually "try on" the meaning structure of a paraplegic (Mezirow, 2000).

Dialectic Process of Transformative Learning

Jack Mezirow's (1991) work reflected his effort to develop a comprehensive theory of adult learning. According to Edward Taylor (1997), Mezirow's theory can be understood as "a linear, though not always stepwise process beginning with a disorienting dilemma, followed by a self-examination of feelings, critical reflection, exploring and planning new roles, negotiating relationships, building confidence, and developing a more inclusive and discriminating perspective" (p. 3).

For every set of attributes describing a point of view in a particular context (thesis), one considers a set of attributes that describe what that point of view might not be (antithesis) in the same context. This consideration of the antithesis is closely related to Sasshi as an approach to analyzing a message, considering alternative interpretations. The process of transformative learning in relation to intercultural interactions can be conceptualized through a dialectic flow of thinking. Transformative learning may be deconstructed into the set of steps (Lucas, 1994) and related to dialectic thinking in the following way:

1. A single extreme disorienting dilemma or a critical accumulation of (smaller) preconceptions (which might surface from dialectic interactions);

2. Critical examination of whole self or bodymind—identity, emotion, spirituality, and action (Wong, 2006) (through inner dialog/dialectic);

3. Critical assessment of an individual's points of view (through inner dialog/dialectic);

4. Critical coreflection on points of view of others, who are involved in the same interaction out of which the disorienting dilemma emerged (this might require careful dialectic inquiry);

5. Further critical coreflection on the meaning structures that underlie the alternative points of view (this too might require careful dialectic inquiry);

6. Revision of assumptions, perspectives, and expectations to resolve the dilemma and accommodate new points of view relative to a new meaning structure (inner dialog/dialectic);

7. Action on the new meaning structure (may include dialectic inquiry);

8. Development of competence and self-confidence based on the new meaning structure and associated points of view (requires both, dialectic interactions and inner dialectic inquiry); and

9. Return to step 6 if the disorienting dilemma has not been resolved or to step 1 if a new disorienting dilemma is generated.

Critical self-examination is implicit in most of the above steps. It requires an ongoing inquiry into one's points of view and their roots in one's meaning structure.

Everything Flows: Panta Rei

Dialectics maybe deconstructed into a framework of schemata broadly divided into those that deal with motion, form, relationships, and a metaformal level (Basseches, 1980, 1984). The *motion*-focused dialectic supports the view of reality as a process; everything changes. It gives priority to change when interpreting the meaning of events. The TAS spiral is a conceptual tool for understanding the nature of this motion. The *form*-oriented schemata are about recognition of the context-sensitivity of points of view as forms and the process of contextualization itself within a broader organizational hierarchy of systems. The meaning or value of an idea is relative to its context, but when taken out of context, this might cause an incongruity. *Relationship* schemata are about considering and conceptualizing the nature of relationships between other dialectic schemata. These relationships may be viewed as dynamic both within the system of thinking and between the system and its context. The relationships drive fundamental change in thinking (Murchison, 1973, p. 252). They define a phenomenon. The *whole* comprises the phenomena with their internal dynamics and relationships between the dynamics. The antithesis of the dialectic approach involves that of never changing from holding one *correct* position and regarding all others as incorrect, whether or not anyone else agrees. The essential difference is that the dialectic includes the process of synthesis, which results in new points of view. As soon as a synthesis emerges as a thesis, the process of synthesis begins again. A point of view (thesis) is contextualized both in form and in relevant relationships between participants in a dialogic negotiation. The dialectic approach to revising a point of view considers these relationships as essential to evolving a more inclusive, differentiated, and integrated point of view. The process is inclusive of the thesis and antithesis. It first differentiates them and then integrates them into a new form, the synthesis.

The motion-oriented, form-oriented, and relationship-oriented schemata are integrated within the *metaformal* schemata. They involve recognition of disorienting dilemmas and their resolution within an evaluative framework that is based on a set of values, which derive from this process. A value that emerges from the dialectic is the significance of contradiction and hence its role in the process of transformation. The adoption of dialectic thinking is self-reinforcing. The dialectic thinker is distinguished by the way he/she actively locates disorienting dilemmas and regards them in a constructive manner. Frequently, preconceptions result in changes to point of view, but after an accumulation of such changes, or an infrequent, extreme disorienting dilemma, a transformation of meaning structure might be triggered. George Novak (1940) described this as the dialectic law of change from quantity into quality, sometimes named *leaping development* (Wan-Chi Wong, 2006).

Transformational learning may be visualized as the experience of following a trajectory, much like rafting through the white water in rapids, in which there are overlapping contradictions. As the learner synthesizes a new thesis from a former thesis and antithesis, it is as much a challenge of "letting go" of the previous thesis, as it is to accept the new thesis (Kosok, 1972). It is uncomfortable to *let go*.

As reflected in Figure 3.3, the motion of the dialectic through recurrences of the TAS cycle follows a trajectory that continues the process of reviewing, revising, and refining points of view and eventually meaning structures. This reflects a dialectic epistemology of active conceptualization of ideas rather than just accumulation of facts without any critical analysis (Moss, Girard, & Haniford, 2006).

In the context of intercultural learning, this dialectic spiral may trigger recurrence of further TAS sequences in various directions that correspond to the differing viewpoints of multiple cultures. Such patterns mirror the complexity of multicultural interactions in the real world.

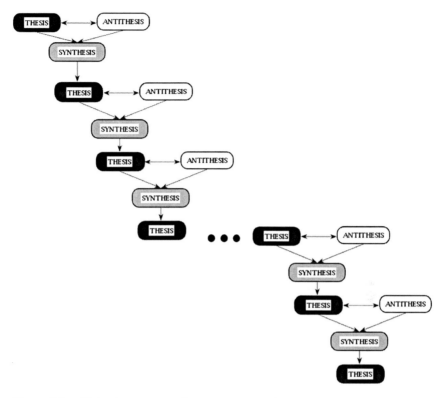

Figure 3.3.   Dialectic processes shape our perspectives.

In intercultural learning, as we are developing perspective conscious-ness, it is important to realize that our perspectives and those of others are continually changing. It is the relationships between the dynamics of our respective perspectives, intrapersonally and interpersonally, that define our perspectives. Therefore, during the development of ICC com-petence, it can be misleading to draw conclusions about individual per-spectives at a particular instant in time. This is because such perspectives are contextual and temporary, emerging from the interactions between the processes of their formation. What we will see in a perspective is a fleeting instantiation of something that is continually changing, however slowly. As a result, dialectic thinking is essential for developing ICC com-petence and successful global learning.

An important characteristic of the learner is the ability to understand the premises for and consequences of a paradox. Another way to view this is for the intercultural learner to be able to understand opposing perspectives, whether they involve global or local diversity. The goal of

situational ethics?

intercultural learning is to gain this understanding through dialog and then to find a region somewhere between the extremes. Attainment of a single position is almost impossible, because of being within a dynamic system. One or the other extreme is equally out of reach, because of the unity of extremes. For example, in a multicultural society, it may be possible in the short term to fully satisfy one ethnic group, but in the long term, this can turn out to be a mistake. Keeping every ethnic group in a multicultural society equally happy in the long term is utopian because of internal and external dynamics. The best we can hope for, when dealing with opposite perspectives, is to remain in a region of relative agreement. Finding the point of perfect agreement is an illusory quest.

INTEGRATING CULTURAL DIALECTICS

Cultures can be analyzed in terms of their characteristics (Scott, Mortimer, & Aguiar, 2006) and some of these may be viewed as dialectic opposites. For example, in relation to social hierarchies, at one extreme, some cultural groups may have closely observed and rigid hierarchies, while at the other extreme some may be highly egalitarian. Dialectical thinking provides a framework for the dialogic coconstruction of shared meanings within the continuum between the opposites. This often requires creative thinking. Consider the case of the American husband and Japanese wife with a new baby. In Japan it is usual to have the baby sleep between the parents, while for the North American husband the expectation is for the baby to sleep on its own. Rather than adopting or imposing one or the other extreme within this dialectic, having the mother sleep between the baby and father turned out to be an acceptable compromise (Lindner, 2006a). Such a dialectical approach is most likely to occur when we adopt mutual respect between cultures.

Figure 3.4 illustrates how Judith N. Martin and Thomas K. Nakayama (1999) arrived at the dialectic perspective of culture and communication. The four initial paradigms, represented as four quadrants (Figure 3.4.), are framed by Gibson Burrell and Gareth Morgan's (1988) view of the nature of social science and the nature of society. The nature of society is viewed in terms of order—stability and regulation, and conflict—critical views of oppression and change. The nature of social science is considered as being on a continuum between the subjectivist and objectivist worldviews: from reality being internal and making meaning about the world around us to belief in an external world in which the researcher and the researcher's object of study can be separated.

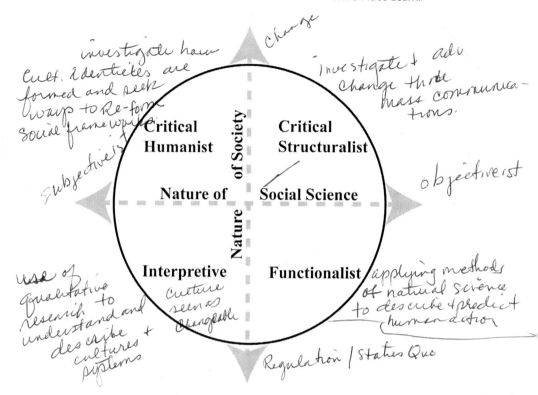

Figure 3.4.   Four paradigms of dialectic thinking relative to continua for the nature of society and the nature of social science.

The four paradigms, *Critical Humanist, Critical Structuralist, Interpretive,*
and *Functionalist,* although represented as four distinct quadrants relative
to the continua of the *Nature of Society* and the *Nature of Social Science,*
should be considered as somewhat irregular and permeable (Figure 3.4).
They have different defining characteristics and some shared properties.
The Nature of Social Science continuum ranges from *Subjectivist* on the
left to *Objectivist* on the right, while the Nature of Society continuum
varies from the *Scholarship of Radical Change* at the top to the *Scholarship of
Regulation* at the bottom. The following is a brief description of these
paradigms, based on Martin and Nakayama's (1999) work reported in
Thinking Dialectically About Culture and Communication. The *Functionalist*
paradigm reflects an attempt to apply methods of the natural sciences to
the investigation of culture and communication, with the goal of
describing and potentially predicting human actions. On the other hand,
Interpretive researchers typically use qualitative research methods in an
attempt to understand and describe the world, cultures and systems of

communication that surround them. Culture is seen as socially constructed, changeable, and uneven within a single nation. Culture both shapes and is articulated through communication (Burrell & Morgan, 1988; Martin & Nakayama, 1999).

Recognition of the importance of understanding contexts, the role of power and the relevance of intercultural interactions in daily professional and personal lives is brought into the play in two additional paradigms. Critical humanism and critical structuralism aim to investigate/explain the influence of power and contextual factors on communication and culture. *Critical Humanists* regard reality as socially constructed (as in the interpretive world view) but at the same time they see human conscience as dominated by social hierarchy and material conditions; culture becomes a site of contesting various communication meanings, not just a variable. Critical humanists are concerned with understanding how cultural identities are constructed in intercultural settings and investigating ways in which it is possible to go beyond or reconfigure existing social frameworks. *Critical Structuralists* regard reality from an objectivist point of view; their way of investigating and advocating change is based on the significance of established structures and conditions that facilitate opportunities for cultural interactions. Both critical humanists and critical structuralists appear not to focus on ICC and interpersonal interactions but on mass communication and popular culture expression (Martin & Nakayama, 1999).

Martin and Nakayama (1999) provided detailed analysis of the four paradigms (Figure 3.4.) by constructing an argument that there are at least four positions from which ways of thinking about ICC can be challenged: Liberal Pluralism; Interparadigmatic Borrowing; Multiparadigmatic Collaboration; and Dialectic Perspective (Figure 3.5). *Liberal Pluralism* acknowledges values of each paradigm, but it does not examine the interconnectedness of these paradigms. For example, it does not provide a framework for how ideas from one paradigm might enrich understanding of research from other paradigms. Researchers who adopt the *Interparadigmatic Borrowing* position, although firmly set in one of the paradigms, can investigate and recognize contributions from other paradigms and integrate some questions and ideas into their own research. The *Multiparadigmatic Collaboration* is based on a view that any isolated research paradigm is limited and attempts to make explicit contributions

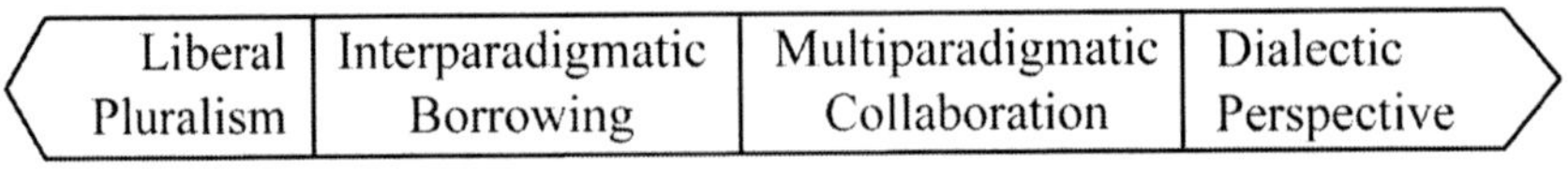

Liberal Pluralism	Interparadigmatic Borrowing	Multiparadigmatic Collaboration	Dialectic Perspective

Figure 3.5.   Four positions in the dialectic continuum of paradigms.

of each paradigm when researching the same question. It can be seen as research with multiple points of reference and seems to be an appropriate paradigm for research by multicultural teams. The *dialectic perspective* transcends the notion of holding multiple points of view, even contradictory ones. It recognizes essential contradictions of human nature and inherent dynamics of overcoming them. In the dialectic approach to ICC, culture and communication are considered relative to the foreground: environment and power relationships. Martin and Nakayama (1999) formulate some of the ICC dialectics, which can serve as a basic framework for conversations about ICC among interacting individuals from both very similar and very different cultures. In the context of cage painting these dialectics (introduced in chapter 1) may be described in the following way:

Cultural-Individual Dialectic: In cage painting, both individual and cultural characteristics play a significant role. The norms and behaviors of the group and individuals' behavioral traits are dynamically related and sometimes at odds or in a state of tension. Everyone expects to be recognized as a member of his/her cultural group and as an individual, even though these may be contradictory in terms of some characteristics (Collier, 1991).

Personal/Social-Contextual Dialectic: Behavioral characteristics are dependent on the context; they change with the context. Therefore, cage painting will be affected by contextual factors of the environment. With the use of communication technologies, this dialectic is becoming even more pronounced because of the contextual differences (inter-contextual distance). For example, global collaborators communicating between hemispheres (e.g. between Bangalore, India, and Wichita, Kansas) need to take into account the fact that they may be in work and home contexts as they paint cages. A person at work in India, in the morning is rested and starting his/her day while a person in Wichita, Kansas might be at home and very tired at the end of a long day.

History/Past and Present/Future Dialectic: There is a need to focus simultaneously on the past and the present to understand ICC. Past is always interpreted from the present position. Dialectic perspective supports consideration of the processes involved and recognizes that power relationships are affected by this dialectic. The cage bars that capture the historical perspective of individuals from colonized/occupied group and colonizers/occupiers will affect their perspective of the present and their future aspirations.

Privilege-Disadvantage Dialectic: Each person or cultural group can have both privileges and disadvantages, depending on the context; sometimes the one trait can be simultaneously a privilege and a disadvantage. This directly affects power relationships, which in turn will significantly influence success of cage painting. Being an immigrant is often a disadvantage because of lack of acceptance. At the same time, it is a privilege because of the knowledge and perspectives that one gains about one's own culture and the culture of one's new home.

Differences-Similarities Dialectic: In ICC it is important to recognize significance of both difference and similarity. Effective cage painting builds on similarities and respects differences. For example, although many Australians and Americans share a European heritage and speak English, their cultures are distinct. It is also important to notice that differences and similarities can coexist in intercultural interactions. Similarities can serve as common ground which is an entrée to the third place processes.

Static-Dynamic Dialectic: Culture and communication may vary between being static or in flux; both static and dynamic aspects will affect intercultural interactions. When paying a return visit after a long period to a country, many aspects of culture may have changed. For example, expatriates returning home after a long period may experience a culture shock because the culture of their home country has evolved. Meanwhile the inhabitants may be oblivious to changes that have happened very slowly.

We can think about dialectics as being a lens through which we can view and analyze the complexities and dynamics of intercultural interactions. There are no simple answers in terms of synthesis from dilemmas, but rather we need to recognize multiple, contradictory viewpoints, and be able to search for ways of successfully interacting in such circumstances. We need to view things in, "processual, relational and holistic terms" (Martin & Nakayama, 1999, p. 67). The above list is an initial set of dialectics that Martin and Nakayama offered in order to initiate a somewhat structured entry into dialectic way of thinking about cultures and ICC. As we interact with different people, we are continuously and simultaneously expressing our positions on many intersecting dialectic continua. In the language of cage painting, this means we are continually painting and repainting bars. As our student John said, *The paint never dries.*

For example, dialectic continua could form the basis for initiating cage painting with a stranger. These examples of dialectics should facilitate understanding the perspectives of others. By allowing oneself to think along the continuum of various dialectics, consideration of multiple perspectives, sometimes contradictory to those strongly held by an individual, will receive appropriate attention. This approach could help resolve disorienting dilemmas and develop shared points of view in a dialogic context.

interpretive

HERMENEUTIC ATTITUDE AND ACTION

The second major component of the theory supporting third place intercultural transformative learning is *hermeneutic attitude and action*. The three processes of (1) critical reflection and coreflection, (2) epistemic cognition, and (3) holistic mindfulness, each inform hermeneutic attitude and consequent action. Transformative learning theory articulates the changes taking place during intercultural learning as a result of these three constituent processes. Reflective inquiry and action are needed to deal with the dialectic between new information and the individual's "foreknowledge, preconceptions or prejudices" (Gadamer, 1981, p. 111) as part of a hermeneutic cycle (Moss et al., 2006). In particular, the three processes are applied to being aware of and taking into account one's own perspective and further to challenge and transform that perspective as one participates in the dialogic negotiation of meaning with others. This requires a *hermeneutic attitude* (Gadamer, 1987), or the courage to expose and transform beliefs and attitudes (meaning structure) in order to arrive at coherence with those of others. Drawing on critical social theory, third place intercultural learning requires critical hermeneutic consciousness to overcome the effects of unequal power that often shape beliefs and attitudes.

Critical Reflection and Coreflection

Original writings on reflection are attributed to John Dewey's (1910/ 1933) exploration and conceptualization of thinking in his book *How We Think* (e.g., Rodgers, 2002). Carol Rodgers summarized Dewey's writings about reflection in four criteria which we broaden and adapt into *six guiding principles for reflecting in intercultural learning environments:* (1) reflection is a dialectic meaning making process, (2) reflection is a rigorous way of thinking, (3) reflection is a seed of coreflection, (4) reflection is guided by a set of attitudes, (5) reflection is not by definition critical, and (6) reflection-in-action is called for. Reflective discourse in the context of transformative learning theory is based upon these six principles derived from Dewey's framework. We now elaborate on each of these principles.

Reflection is a dialectic meaning making process from experiences, where (a) experiences are very broadly conceived as *interactions* between oneself and the world and (b) making sense of new experiences is based on one's own past experiences; a *continuity* or "bridge of meaning that connects one experience to the next" (Rodgers, 2002, p. 850).

Reflection is a rigorous way of thinking with its roots in scientific inquiry; it can be conceptualized as cycling through certain phases: an initial experience/exploration, (spontaneous) interpretation, naming a problem or generating a question, considering a plausible explanation, subsequently testing the selected assumption in a new situation, interpretation, generating a new question, considering another explanation, testing a new assumption and so on, by analogy to the dialectic flow.

Reflection is a seed of coreflection: Dewey (1944) recognized that explicating one's point of view to others requires some understanding of others' perspectives; "One has to assimilate, imaginatively, something of another's experience in order to tell him intelligently of one's own experience" (p. 6); is a key part of ascending the levels of cage painting (Figure 2.7). Collaborative reflection (Figure 1.5) may be described as a dialogic (collaborative) critical thinking process either active or tacit, involving both cognitive and affective interactions. It affirms one's experience; it informs that experience in relation to the others' points of view and it might instigate further (collaborative) inquiry (Rodgers, 2002).

Reflection is guided by a set of attitudes, some of which have been introduced by Dewey, and some either introduced or elaborated upon by others: whole-heartedness, directness with self-awareness (without self-absorption), open-mindedness, responsibility, readiness, mindfulness (Langer, 1989), and bodymindfulness (Nagata, 2007).

Reflection is not by definition critical. Critical reflection is a deeper, more intense, probing form of reflection. It occurs when we identify and challenge the criteria that define how things should be judged; when we learn how certain socially-valued protocols and expressions or appreciation came to constitute the standard or norm. This may involve power-distance analysis of the context within which this process happens. Origins of critical reflection belong to the Frankfurt School of Critical Social Theory and are closely related to Freire's (1968/1970) consideration of power relationships and the pedagogy of the oppressed.

Reflection-in-action is called for. The most common interpretation of *reflection* is as *reflection-on-action*: reflection on actions after they have occurred. To be mindful, by taking into account an interlocutor's points of view and the context, a more immediate *reflection-in-action* is called for, even if it is believed that this will impede or paralyze the process that is in action (Schön, 1983), such as teaching or communicating. Carol Rodgers (2002) argued that even if action is slowed down, reflection-in-action is needed to become cognizant of *tacit* knowledge (Polanyi, 1967; Selman, 1988) or the meaning structure that underpins the interactants' points of view. The key, according to Dewey (1910/1933), is "being able to select

to "change your mind" persuade?

and apply just what is needed when it is needed" (p. 65) which undoubtedly reminds us of Enryo-Sasshi type of interactions.

Reflective discourse in the context of transformative learning theory. While Dewey's (1910/1933, 1944) work is about the nature of reflection, Donald Schön's (1983, 1987) contributions focused on the nature of reflective practice/action. Reflective discourse involves critical inquiry into assumptions and interpretations in search for common understanding or justification of an interpretation or belief. It is a process in which a person is facilitating his/her own understanding of an experience through an active dialog in a very broad sense. According to Jack Mezirow (2000), a dialog may be an interaction with another person, within the group, or with an author, in effect, through thinking about an event in the author's book or similarly with an artist when interpreting a piece of art (Dewey, 1910/1933). In an intercultural learning environment, this process focuses on active interaction with other people.

Metacognition and Epistemic Cognition

There are three levels of cognitive processing: *cognition, metacognition,* and *epistemic cognition* (Kitchener, 1983). Cognition is a single instance of a learning process or strategy that is (hopefully) optimal for a given context, perhaps within one culture. Metacognitive thinking involves active control over the process of thinking (Flavell, 1979) and refers to people's abilities to monitor their own thinking and levels of understanding. Learning practices congruent with metacognitive approaches include those that focus on mindfulness, sense-making, self-assessment, and reflection and coreflection on what worked and what needs to be improved (e.g., Schoenfeld, 1992). Furthermore, the practice of metacognitive thinking helps transfer learning to new contexts (Burgoon, Berger, & Waldron, 2000; Langer, 1997). *Systems thinking (Fifth Discipline)*

When two individuals, from different cultures, are coconstructing meaning through dialog and reflection, they become critically aware of their own and each other's meaning structures and the effect of these on their interpretations of each other's point of view. If there is a significant level of dissonance in their interpretations, one or both individuals may start to re-examine the limits and certainty of their knowledge, and his/her way of knowing: *epistemic cognition* (Kitchener, 1983; Mezirow, 2000). This epistemic cognitive processing, which induces alteration of meaning structures is an instance of transformative learning. It may result in new, hybrid ways of knowing (syntheses of the dialectic) that transcend those of each of the individual's cultures.

Holistic Mindfulness

Complementary to metacognitive thinking in the sphere of ICC is metacommunication and heightened awareness of the process through mindfulness (Alagic, Gibson, & Rimmington, 2007). *Mindfulness* involves thoughtful processing of communicated information, context sensitivity, awareness of perspectives, and recognition of distinct representations (Langer, 1997) and represents the opposite of *mindlessness* in communication. Mindlessness is characterized by automatic behaviors from a single perspective. Nagata (2006) took the concept to a more holistic level and defined *bodymindfulness* as "the process of attending to all aspects of the bodymind in order to grasp the holistic personal meaning of an internal event and to use the resultant understanding to communicate skillfully" (p. 46). It involves both intrapersonal and interpersonal abilities, being familiar with one's own inner states, and paying attention to the feelings of others (Taylor, 2000). This is important during face-to-face interactions, when information about emotions and feelings is shared nonverbally. It is essential to be aware that this component is missing during online communication. An attempt needs to be made to compensate for this to maintain an approximation of bodymindfulness within the text- or voice-based environment, for example through the use of emoticons.

Holistic mindfulness strengthens reflection-in-action by involving self-awareness. It brings to the foreground knowledge that is usually tacit or implicit (Schön, 1983). It is awareness of such knowledge that positions us for transformation of our perspectives, *going over the edge*. Edge is about confronting our assumptions in the face of a disorienting experience related to our cultural beliefs. Such beliefs that we hold dear, may work against us and serve the interest of others. For example, meaning structure that arises from the enculturation of early schooling may be ethnocentric. Arnold Mindell (1990) explained, "Edges are names for the experience of the confinement, for the limitations in awareness, for the boundaries of your identity" (p. 71).

Edges are exposed by critical reflection (Wong, 2006) and are brought into focus by holistic mindfulness. They are reached when we confront our inner assumptions, which are at odds with our current experiences. Dialectically speaking, the act of going over the edge involves letting go of a thesis, considering an antithesis, and seeking a synthesis. Wan-chi Wong identified this as preparation for change. Our personal growth as learners may be marked by the desire for more transformative learning experiences at the boundaries/edges of our assumptions about the world.

SYSTEMS VIEW OF THIRD PLACE INTERCULTURAL LEARNING

To better understand the process of cage painting and its role in third place learning processes, it is useful to refer to the literature on the third place (space), mainly the work of Homi K. Bhabha (1994). The third place may be conceptualized as, a path through hybridity between two viewpoints or related meaning structures, of qualitative change; a result of effective cage painting. It contrasts with intrinsic, isolated consideration of one's viewpoint. Applying this idea to individual interactants from different cultures, we paint cages with reference to another person through a process of coreflection. This is accomplished by thinking in terms of being able to observe our own cage as we are observing the cage of the other person.

Third place processes may also be described as cage painting facilitated by its interactants to reach beyond cage painters' shared thresholds. As Bhabha (1994) says,

> It is that Third Space, though unrepresentable in itself, which constitutes the discursive conditions of enunciation that ensure that the meaning and symbols of culture have no primordial unity or fixity; that even the same signs can be appropriated, translated, rehistorisized and read anew. (p. 55)

Facilitating the third place processes involves: (1) encouraging a socialization phase, (2) the cultivation of *Enryo-Sasshi* and multiple perspectives, (3) dialectic thinking, (4) cognizance of the effect of power distance, (5) ensuring everyone has a voice, (6) introducing disorienting dilemmas to stimulate threshold thinking, (7) cultivating holistic mindfulness, and (8) encouraging critical reflective inquiry through guiding questions as part of a metacognitive apprenticeship within a social constructivist paradigm. Expected outcomes may include: *Perspective taking*—the development of consciousness of one's own perspective and that of others, and *Sasshi listening*—active consideration of alternatives.

To summarize, intercultural learning and third place processes relative to existing theories focus on the dialectic and dynamic nature of learners, the process of learning and the context of learning. This type of learning is located at the intersection of critical social theory and social constructivist learning theory (Crotty, 2003; Kincheloe, 2005; National Research Council, 2000). These theories support the development of multiple perspectives through dialogic coconstruction of meaning by a community of learners: students, instructors and experts with various inherent p relationships. Intercultural learning requires the cultivation of c

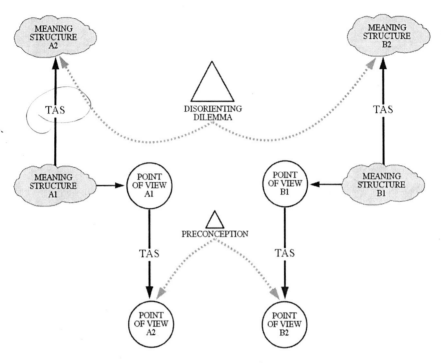

Figure 3.6.   Third place learning: dialectic process of altering point of view or meaning structure.

thinking, mindfulness and that all learners have a voice. Figure 3.6 above captures the interplay of dialectic thinking and transformative learning in response to encountering intercultural differences that may be at the level of points of view ($\triangle$) or meaning structures ($\triangle$). In the latter case, the difference cannot be resolved by simply altering point(s) of view. Rather, the dialectic inquiry needs to be applied to achieve a deeper understanding, which may cause a change in one or both interactants' meaning structures. This corresponds to the second loop in Chris Argyris' (1999) double-loop learning model for organizations being applied to intercultural interactions.

The challenge now is to use this theoretical positioning to inform the design of intercultural learning environments as this is integrated into curricula. It is our hope that, collaborating facilitators will give careful consideration to the challenges of the environment design, for the benefit of their respective students. The next section presents an outline and guiding principles for the design of appropriate learning environments.

LEARNING ENVIRONMENT DESIGN

An implicit challenge of social constructivist learning in culturally diverse or intercultural contexts is the need for successful cage painting in order to accomplish other relevant learning objectives. Our learning environment design (Figures 3.7a-d.) suggests ways to facilitate cage painting as a means of accomplishing the learning objectives. It was motivated by global learning experiences described in chapter 4 and the instructional design of open and e-learning environments (Hannafin et al., 1999). A distinguishing characteristic of this environment is that the learners are located in different countries or in culturally diverse contexts. The dialog among learners may be facilitated with modern communication technologies within the situated learning paradigm. This cognitive apprenticeship type of learning environment is contextualized to capture the twofold goal: completion of an authentic task and successful ICC.

This environment should be designed so that the learners are exposed to a context that precipitates the development of perspective consciousness. One way to accomplish this is to provide a multicultural team of

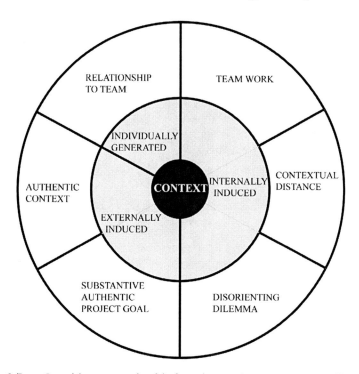

Figure 3.7a.   Cognitive apprenticeship learning environment: Externally and internally imposed and individually generated contexts with their instantiations.

learners with a project goal that is authentic in terms of the content area being studied and that is substantial enough that one person alone cannot accomplish it. An authentic project for a mechanical engineering course would be to develop a design or prototype for a company or client that is outside the context of the educational institution. Being required to achieve a project goal collaboratively will place importance on effective ICC.

The cultural backgrounds of participants can affect meaning making about course content as well as communication in general (McLoughlin, 2002). The design needs to include appropriate communication technologies preferably with multiple and redundant modes of communication (Collins, 1991). The focus of this communication is social and professional interaction for dialogic coconstruction of meaning. For this dialog to be effective, significant attention needs to ensure that the participants feel comfortable sharing perspectives in a well-designed learning environment (Edmundson, 2007; Wang & Reeves, 2007) or, in other words, facilitating third place processes.

Intercultural learning in this kind of learning environment is an activity that can be integrated into the curriculum for different discipline areas. Therefore there will be two types of learning goals, those concerned with the discipline area (e.g., music, engineering, or mathematics) and those associated with intercultural learning. There are two sets of design considerations necessary to facilitate the completion of a project-based learning assignment. Depending on the discipline area, the two sets of goals may be more or less intertwined. Furthermore, designers of these learning environments need to have a heightened awareness of the effects of culture on pedagogical assumptions, such as power relationships between the learner and instructor.

COGNITIVE APPRENTICESHIP METHODS

As already mentioned, the learning environment design introduced here shares characteristics with open and e-learning environments that are distinct from directed learning environments. It is best situated within both a problem- and multicultural team-based context that is authentic and meaningful as preparation for work in the discipline area in a global and multicultural context. The problem should be complex and substantive so as to require teamwork for successful completion. The goals and information about the project need to be ill-defined and ill-structured so as to promote autonomous and self-directed learning for the team members. As the project proceeds, the learners will need to develop their own ICC

This type of team is operating in Doc. of minn groups. at McCormick,

heuristic and project strategies, evaluate their progress, and make decisions. They need a sufficiently safe environment within which it is acceptable to make mistakes both in terms of the discipline area and in terms of communication. To accomplish these aims, the four cognitive apprenticeship methods for an open learning environment (Hannafin et al., 1999) have been adapted to this learning environment. They are the context, resources, processes, and scaffolding (Figure 3.7a-d). We will consider each of these in more detail.

Context

By the nature of social-constructivism, learning outcomes cannot be achieved through direct instruction. Therefore an appropriate context (Figure 3.7a) is critical. The effects of externally imposed, externally induced, and individually generated conditions together shape this context. The imposed discipline-based project goal and globally distributed or local, multicultural team should lead to the completion of the project and the achievement of intercultural learning goals. The global or multicultural context induces a contextual distance between learners and may result in disorienting dilemmas that challenge the learner to generate circumstances, which lead to a resolution. For example, in a project that involves individuals with different conceptions of punctuality (precise versus flexible), they may negotiate small windows of time (say 15 minutes) for beginning a meeting instead of precise times, such as 10 o'clock sharp.

Resources

The instructors' collaborative efforts in designing the learning environment and facilitating the process may serve as an example for the learner's cognitive apprenticeship behaviors. Other resources are of a physical nature (Figure 3.7b). Associated with each learning environment design will be project infrastructure specific to the discipline area. The challenge is to recognize the differences in infrastructure between locations in a distributed project and work on accommodating any differences that might impede the project's successful completion. Similar attention needs to be given to the other essential physical resource: the communication technologies. For example, in a music project between two countries, if one has advanced project infrastructure and high bandwidth communication

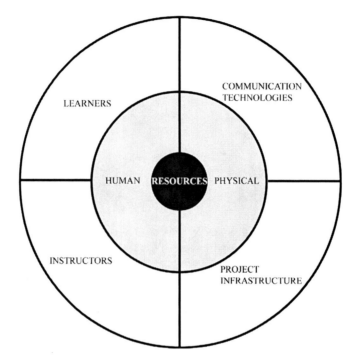

Figure 3.7b.   Cognitive apprenticeship learning environment: Resources with its components and their instantiations

technologies and the other has incompatible or aging infrastructure and
communication technology, then creativity and imagination will become
essential for accomplishing collaborative results.

Processes

In addition to cognitive processes, such as organizing, integrating,
generating, testing and others, the learning environments being
described here will require global reach or local cultural diversity
(Figure 3.7c). The immediacy of synchronous interactions over vast distances or even the reliability of a medium for regular asynchronous
interactions using modern communication technologies provides the
physical conditions for the third place processes in either global or local
intercultural learning activities.

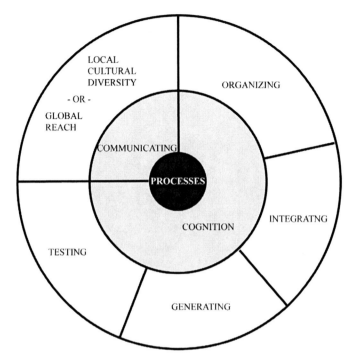

Figure 3.7c. Cognitive apprenticeship learning environment:
Processes with its components and their instantiations.

Scaffolding

Cognitive apprenticeship provides conditions for conceptual, proce-
dural and strategic scaffolding; processes through which third place processes and intercultural learning activities are sustained (Figure 3.7d).
Scaffolding provides guidance for learners on what issues to consider, and
how to analyze and approach the project's constituent tasks.

Even if the learners have previous experience with reflective practices,
the learning environment under consideration here might require more
emphasis on reflection guided by instructors due to potentially significant
differences in understanding each other's context. By metacognitive
reflection on the project, collaborative engagement and considering how
these two affect progress on the project and intercultural learning,
learners will become aware of their own perspective and its effect on their
perspective of others.

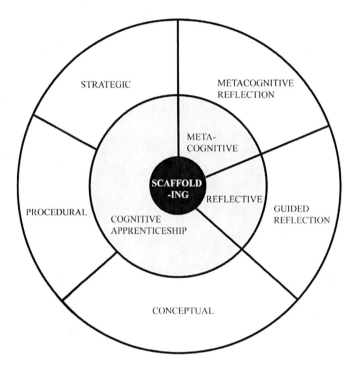

Figure 3.7d.   Cognitive apprenticeship learning environment: Scaffolding with its components and their instantiations.

NEED FOR AN APPROPRIATE CONCEPTUAL FRAMEWORK

Promoting dialectic thinking and negotiation about cultural characteristics is at odds with the dimension-based model of cultures (e.g., Hofstede, 1980), which conforms more closely to the *banking* model of learning. As with the example of trying to apply continental-scale climatic averages to the prediction of daily weather for a town or village, information about national cultural dimensions has limited value at the level of the individual in the specific context within a given nation. It is not a tool that will help much in the situation of two people immersed in their home cultures but interacting via global reach.

The cultural basis of the cage painting model is analogous to the cultural dimension model, except that it acknowledges that there are many attributes (cage bars) of varying importance in different contexts, and that they are continually changing over time and between contexts. In other words, we cannot *learn* a cage and then apply it to a context; we cannot paint cages out of a context. It is learned within a context and continues to be learned. It is not predefined, but is emergent. It does not fit with a banking or transmission model of learning; it matches better with a transformative model embedded within a critical pedagogical framework.

As already mentioned, the learning environment described here might be viewed as comprising two essential components: the means to connect people of different cultures and the requirement to achieve some common goals through collaboration in a team-based project. This goal relates to the content area of the course or program as distinct from the goal of improving ICC competence. So the instructor in business or engineering will want learners to achieve a goal such as writing a business plan plus to achieve improved ICC. However, one more ingredient is needed. It is the role of the educational designer to create situations in which the participants will experience some disorienting dilemma, cognitive dissonance, or culture shock. For instance, in a global business project the participants will need to deal with different currencies, economic policies, laws, ethics, work practices, customer preferences, units of measurement, or attitudes toward quality. Failure to understand and adapt to any or all of these issues could result in catastrophe for a real business venture. For a participant with little or no prior experience of having to collaborate with others, whose perspectives differ markedly, just one such issue could constitute a disorienting dilemma.

Two products of the twentieth century that have created the opportunity for more people to interact interculturally are relatively more affordable jet air travel and the Internet. The latter allows participants to stay within their home context and to meet in cyberspace. From the perspective of the business manager, who seeks to lower costs, this is very attractive, because it allows people working as part of a global team to avoid travel but still remain in touch on a regular basis. However, this is a double-edged sword. On the other side, the participants in such an arrangement must deal with intercultural differences in the communication, without the benefit of physical contextualization. What is the cost of miscommunication? The challenge of improving intercultural learning is amplified when participants are globally distributed. As educators, we can provide environments for learners to improve their ICC without the need for travel or exchange programs, although the latter are definitely beneficial, if they are available.

There is a plethora of Internet-based communication tools available to facilitate third place processes in a learning environment with globally distributed participants. They include the telephone, e-mail, interactive messaging, threaded discussions, Voice over Internet Protocol (VoIP) and IP-based videoconferencing. Each has its advantages and disadvantages. The viability of each tool depends on the available bandwidth. Each requires different preparation and communication strategies. For instance, if a class in Wichita has a phone conference scheduled with someone in Nigeria, the participants need to be encouraged to formulate questions prior to the phone conference and to participate actively, taking notes and reflecting and then prepare some shared artifact that is the result of their collaboration. An important strategy is to be mindful of factors that affect the availability of a reliable connection and to have available alternative ways to connect. For example, when using videoconferencing, instant messaging or SMS (Short Message Service) can be used as a supplementary backup if the videoconference connection is disrupted.

SUMMARY: WHERE WE ARE AND WHERE WE ARE GOING

In this chapter we provided the philosophical and theoretical underpinnings of the intercultural and global communication competences presented in chapter 1 and the cage painting learning environment described in chapter 2. Underlying these are critical pedagogy, multiculturism, and social constructivist learning theories. Facilitation of the third place learning supports the application of cage painting for improvement of ICC (Figure 3.8).

The conditions for the Third Place Processes and their outcomes were presented. The third place processes can stimulate transformative learning that is embedded within a dialectic flow of thinking. Hermeneutic attitude and action are coupled with a set of cultural dialectics and integrated into the overall learning design. The learning environment presented here features a cognitive and metacognitive apprenticeship that allows the learner to emulate, adopt and to autonomously evolve strategies for transformative learning in response to preconceptions and disorienting dilemmas. These considerations lend support to the ideas and strategies presented in chapters 1 and 2. In the next chapter, we explore the application of these ideas to global learning. Some lessons are derived from case studies and examples of global learning over a 6-year period. These can serve as a guide for those readers, who wish to integrate global learning experiences into their courses or programs.

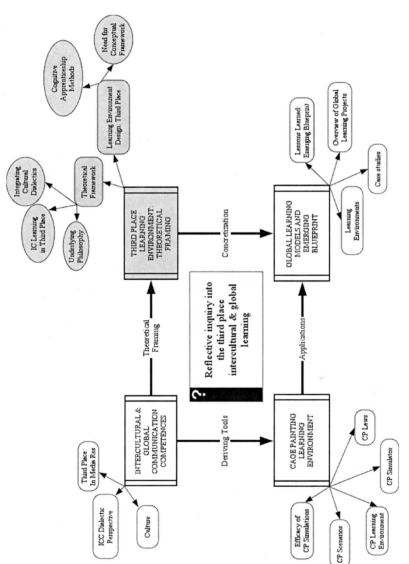

Figure 3.8. Searching for the quintessence of the Third Place Learning.

CHAPTER 4

GLOBAL LEARNING MODELS AND EMERGING BLUEPRINT

The latent learning potential of the world population has been grossly underestimated as a result of prevailing mind-sets that limit the design of interventions to improve the evolution of the global learning environment.

Cavallo (2000)

The increasing interconnectedness, cultural diversity, and interdependence of the world citizens spells out the need for our education systems to intensely cultivate development of intercultural communication (ICC) competences, cultural proficiency and global learning (GL) competences. Chapter 1 elaborates on these competences and establishes a conceptual framework of ICC based on the cage painting metaphor. An important part of application of this metaphor is an ICC heuristic that may help develop multiple perspectives, when interacting with people from cultural groups different from one's own. Chapter 2 describes the Cage Painting Learning Environment (CPLE), which can be used to help learners to acquire and practice the ICC heuristic. Chapter 3 provides philosophical and theoretical underpinnings for the cage painting metaphor presented in chapter 1 and the CPLE described in chapter 2.

In this chapter, we describe the application of a metacognitive apprenticeship to facilitating improvement of ICC as part of either the multicultural classroom or workplace or in the context of GL. To illustrate

Third Place Learning: Reflective Inquiry Into Intercultural and Global Cage Painting
pp. 109–134
Copyright © 2008 by Information Age Publishing

the latter, we then devote our attention to various examples of GL integration into the curriculum in higher education and in K-12 classrooms. We begin by summarizing instructional design elements for CPLE and GL environments and then describe three particular examples—case studies—in more detail. A variety of examples drawn from different disciplines then follows. The earlier examples of these (2002-2004) provided the impetus for development of the CPLE while later examples (2005-) have incorporated the CPLE. Finally the lessons learned from these examples are compiled and an emerging blueprint for design of learning environments is presented. Important features of the blueprint are:

(a) how to integrate ICC or GL into the curriculum in such a way that it becomes a vehicle for learning in the discipline area and developing a global mindset, and

(b) how to facilitate third place transformative learning processes.

LEARNING ENVIRONMENTS

In this book we deliberate on two different types of learning environments both grounded in the same theoretical framework. The first type is the CPLE and the second type is the learning environment that incorporates *global reach*. In addition, to being an independent learning environment for improving ICC strategies, CPLE should be considered a prerequisite or corequisite for global reach-based learning environments (GLE).

Metacognitive Apprenticeship Within the Situated Learning Paradigm

It is challenging to provide an authentic learning environment for improving ICC as part of a metacognitive apprenticeship within the situated learning paradigm. One solution to this challenge is to provide a virtual learning environment (Collins, 1991) as preparation for subsequently developing ICC in a real intercultural exchange either through technology-mediated communication or through direct face-to-face communication and travel. The CPLE provides a virtual environment with an expectation to facilitate metacognitive development of the learner's ability to effectively interact in intercultural circumstances.

An essential feature of the CPLE is that the learner participates in a chat session with the synthetic character, Simea. The chat session is situated within the context having to achieve some goal in collaboration with Simea

(Figure 2.10), while dealing with an unanticipated preconception. The preconception results in misunderstanding or miscommunication, which impedes progress toward the goal. The underlying assumption is that the goal can be achieved only by continuing a chat with Simea and overcoming the preconception (Rimmington, Gibson, & Alagic, 2007). The CPLE design follows the methodology of a metacognitive apprenticeship (Alagic, Yeotis, Rimmington, & Koert, 2003; Collins, Brown, & Newman, 1989; chapter 3, this volume; Hannafin, Land, & Oliver, 1999). The learner proceeds as an apprentice from playing simulations and deriving strategies for developing ICC to mastery in the form of writing new scenarios; from the first learning process (Figure 2.6) to the second learning process depicted in Figure 2.9, and eventually applying these strategies in real-life situations.

"Truth is not born nor is it to be found inside the head of an individual person, it is born between people collectively searching for truth, in the process of their dialogic [and dialectic] interaction" (Bakhtin, 1929/1984, p. 110). The truth about similarities or differences between cultures and their effect on communication is therefore best derived from the experience of contextualized dialog. In metacognitive development of ICCC, the cognitive interplay of context and collaboration is inescapable (Brown, Collins, & Duguid, 1989). Development of the heuristic associated with levels of cage painting (Figure 2.7) is itself a process of acculturation in the form of third place (Bhabha, 1994) transformative learning processes. The contextualization of the ICC development within a scenario makes the ICC heuristic all the more meaningful.

The metacognitive apprenticeship pedagogical approach provides guidance that increases the learner's awareness of cognitive skills and their effectiveness and appropriateness. In the context of ICC this means selecting learning strategies to improve ICC rather than just focusing on the ICC itself (Collins, 1991). This higher level of awareness (Figure 4.1) requires the development of self-regulating skills (Brown, Collins, & Duguid, 1989; Collins et al., 1989; Yeotis, Alagic, & Gibson, 2004). The facilitation of such learning involves metaphorically building steps (Figure 2.7) through Vygotsky's (1978) Zone of Proximal Development. As the learner finds how he/she needs to use different cage painting strategies in different contexts in order to overcome increasingly complex challenges, he/she will develop a deeper understanding of the ICC heuristic. Further, metacognitive skills are fostered by encouraging one to reflect on one's thinking about differences between the learning patterns of a first-time learner and that of an expert (i.e., Simea as an avatar of the scenario author). The metacognitive apprenticeship continues as the experienced player begins authoring new scenarios and in the process adopts Simea's simultaneous *other culture* and *coach* role, which leads to thinking about and

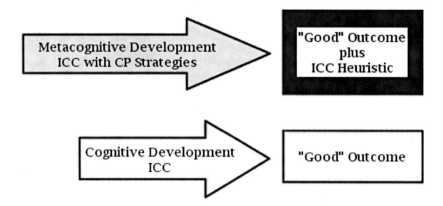

Figure 4.1.   Taking learning a step further: From successfully completing simulations to developing and applying the ICC heuristic.

taking perspectives of people from another culture. As the learner-now-author refines a scenario he/she is encouraged to develop monitoring and correcting (self-regulating) skills.

The learning processes depicted in the Figure 4.2. occur based on the following assumptions:

1.   A substantive, authentic goal to be accomplished,
2.   Multicultural, globally distributed team working toward that goal,
3.   ICC among team members, and
4.   ICC competences arising from CPLE.

One way to think about the design of effective intercultural or GL environments is in terms of CPLE/GLE processes, which will stimulate emergence of the ICC heuristic. That will allow the learner to continually improve his/her cage painting strategies, a precondition for improving Intercultural Communication Competence (ICCC). The GL learning process begins with a goal that is too substantial for an individual to achieve alone and that has authenticity within the discipline domain, (Figure 4.2, right-hand spiral). The substantive nature of the goal will require teamwork and thus collaboration, negotiation and ICC. A high level of authenticity will engage learners more so than goals that do not relate to the discipline area (Alagic, Gibson, & Rimmington, 2007). Development of intercultural and global communication competence will be stimulated further, when the team is multicultural and is globally distributed so that communication is enabled using global reach, made possible by using a variety of communication technologies. The cage painting conceptual

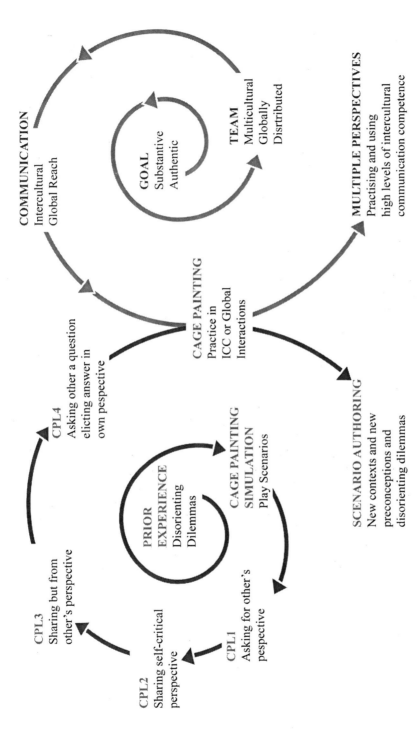

Figure 4.2.   Interplay of the CPLE and GLE processes with corresponding emergent outcomes.

framework helps learners to develop a systematic method for improving their intercultural and global communication. By using the cage painting simulator and relating its scenarios to prior experience, the learner can understand and apply the four cage painting strategies of the ICC heuristic. Further practice and application will lead to sufficient competence for intercultural and global communication and development of multiple perspectives, (Figure 4.2, left-hand spiral). At this level, the learner may contribute new scenarios to the CPLE online scenario repository, thus enriching it as a learning environment for subsequent users.

PRACTICE: INTEGRATING GLOBAL LEARNING

Case Studies

There are three examples of the integration of global intercultural experiences into the curriculum from which new insights emerged. The first example is an online course on ICC competence in which student teams worked with global mentors to develop new scenarios for the CPLE online scenario repository. The second involves the addition of globally distributed project sponsors for senior mechanical engineering design students. The third example concerns a successful GL initiative within one mid-Western school district.

Cage Painting in Action: Intercultural Communication Competence Online Course (Alagic & Rimmington, 2008)

While there are other aspects of global communication and learning that deserve attention, one that is critical for success is *intercultural communication competence* (ICCC). A course devoted to this topic at a theoretical and practical level was developed for graduate students, who wanted to improve their ability to facilitate learning in diverse classrooms or in GL contexts.

The CPLE was utilized as a backbone of this small (nine students) online graduate level course titled: *Intercultural Communication Competence Development*. Quantitative data were collected using both the online courseware tool (courseware statistics about engagement) and CPLE Web site (demographics and performance levels). However, the size of the group inspired researchers to focus on individual stories and therefore implement a qualitative research design, using a critical theoretical perspective as pertinent to this case study (Bogdan & Biklen, 2003; Denzin &

Lincoln, 2005; Merriam, 1998). Qualitative data collected were directly related to gaining an understanding of the cage painting metaphor, constructing personal understanding of the cage painting heuristic and designing scenario-based simulations. The data consist of the following sets: Guided whole class discussions, both structured and unstructured group discussions, individual journaling, cage painting related essays and researchers' notes (online exchanges through social software, for example, Skype, e-mails, and personal observations). Included here are the most relevant, initial findings regarding the CPLE and its effects on students' engagement in the design of new scenarios and generation of corresponding simulations that are now available at http://gl.wichita.edu/CPS/. Due to the emergent nature of qualitative research, the research design remained flexible (Bogdan & Biklen, 2003).

The course content incorporated a thorough discussion of the cultural proficiency continuum (Lindsey, Robins, & Terrell, 2003) aspects of ICCC, the cage painting metaphor, and its application to understanding one's own culture and that of other people. The students first used some cage painting simulations to practice Enryo/Sasshi (Ishii, 1984) thinking about how to choose appropriate responses in a simulated chat session. An important higher-order learning activity involved the students forming into teams to work on writing new scenarios for the CPLE online repository. Each team had a global mentor. The mentors were located in Germany, India, and Qatar. The process of creating a new scenario required the students to adopt multiple perspectives: that of Simea as a model in terms of applying cage painting strategies as well as being of unknown culture; that of the player at each of three levels (Good, Mediocre, and Bad); and that of the educational designer. The latter involves stepping back and examining all aspects of the scenario, such as its context, the goal and the preconception or misunderstanding being considered.

With no intention to make any further generalization, we report the following findings:

(a) Users would like more choices so they can find a better match with their own cage in terms of the area of their professional interest (education, counseling, business)

(b) Teachers participating in this class emphasized that education scenarios were easier for them to follow than, for example, business scenarios; and

(c) A student wanted to propose an alternative for an existing scenario, emphasizing that at some levels "it should be less rude."

When asked, "Design a rubric for evaluating student's success in designing cage painting Simulation," the students focused on evaluating the following: selection of a disorienting dilemma, cage painting levels, scenario writing, and its appropriateness for resolving the disorienting dilemma.

Further analysis of students' discussions seems to confirm an additional recognition of the cognitive modeling capabilities of the CPLE simulator. Analysis of supplemental data supported the interpretation that students recognized the significance of the CP simulations for facilitating critical thinking processes that lead to new ICC knowledge representations. Students who are currently teaching had valuable suggestions about further encouragement of deeper thinking and support for acquiring cultural competence both through the CPLE and in other contexts, such as their classrooms and schools. These suggestions ranged from generating misconceptions about cultural customs that can be topics for writing scenarios to determining how to involve their students in use of the CPLE and follow-up intercultural interactions.

The above findings appear to provide support for the instructional designer's expectations about the CP simulator and online scenario repository as cognitive tools. As a cognitive tool (Derry, 1990; Jonassen & Reeves, 1996), cage painting: (a) facilitates critical thinking that leads to new knowledge representations; (b) supports learners acquisition of skills that are transferable to other contexts; and (c) is both powerful and simple to use.

Mechanical Engineering Senior Design Course (Soschinske, Rimmington, & Alagic, 2006)

Design engineers require many new skills in a world of multicultural, globally distributed teams for projects to design aircraft, cars, or ocean liners, for example. Modern communication technologies make it possible for design teams to interact and share three-dimensional design models in real time from multiple places in the world. This allows such teams to operate on a 24/7 basis (e.g., four 6-hour shifts from Wichita to Sydney to Bangalore to Manchester), shipping data sets as the shifts change. This mode of operation minimizes time-to-market for new products.

Just as the computer network communication protocols have been designed and implemented to allow the hardware and software to function together, work needs to be done to ensure that people can communicate between their cultures competently. To meet this challenge the curricula of engineering programs at one mid-Western university have been revised to integrate systematic approaches to achieving ICCC. Superimposed on this is the additional challenge that much of the communication will involve videoconferencing and text-based media or in other words global reach. We claim that global communication competence (chapter 1, this volume) is called for.

In this example, the capstone design course of a mechanical engineering program was modified to include the opportunity for student teams to develop designs for project sponsors from companies in other countries. Previously, project sponsors were companies located within the same city or within driving distance. In this example, students in Wichita, Kansas, United States worked on a project sponsored by a company in Moscow, Russia. At the same time, a team of students from a university in Moscow worked on a project sponsored by a Wichita company. The potential number of collaborating sites with universities and companies has been expanded to include Bangalore, India and Manchester/Prestwick in the United Kingdom.

The eventual aim, which is a design in progress, is a *Global Design Challenge* in which four teams of four students, each member from a university in Wichita, Moscow, Bangalore, and Manchester, work in a project sponsored by some company. The teams compete to be the first to complete a design to the satisfaction of the sponsoring company. Just as in the real world, minimizing time from the specifications to the prototype or proof-of-concept is critical. The team members communicate using a combination of technologies and in the process they face various ICC challenges. The participating students will gain the additional and valuable learning outcomes of global/ICCC.

A trial of global reach-based learning in the mechanical engineering class during the spring of 2006 yielded some useful findings. Despite exposing the students to industry leaders and the literature on globalization and its implications for engineering design, some remained unconvinced of the relevance of GL. This was also despite news headlines at that time about the high cost of delays to delivery of products stemming from miscommunication along global supply chains. Student behavior was tied closely to grade-percentage allocation, for example in the number of those, who did not keep reflective journals, which were worth 5% of the total assessment for the course. This finding is in agreement with those of Juan C. Lucena (2002) who observed resistance toward learning the nontechnical and more political aspects of GL during such collaboration. The solution may lay in higher allocation of grade-percentage or more meaningful integration of GL and cage painting into the learning activities. That kind of integration would involve learning about cage painting earlier in the course, or in a previous course, and making collaboration with a multicultural team either mandatory or more typical in the available projects. Some coaching for their metacognitive apprenticeship in developing the ICC heuristic (Figure 4.1.) would be essential. It is also important to leave the design specifications more open-ended so that more ICC/negotiation is needed as the design project proceeds. When the outcome is too tightly defined, there will be less need for interaction and hence less opportunity for improving ICC. Although it was not reported in Kurt Albert Soschinske et al. (2006), other factors affected the success of this trial. They included lack of organizational leadership support, minimal availability of the necessary infrastructure, the lack of a well-established relationship between faculty at each institution and insufficient time for students to practice and reflect on cage painting, using the CPLE.

Rwanda Alive at Maize High School: Painting Cages (Rimmington & Bever-Goodvin, 2005)

In 2004 one district initiative to incorporate GL into the curriculum resulted in an opportunity for selected senior high school students to interact with students, experts, indigenous people and wild life officials from the country of Rwanda. A doctoral graduate, who had personal GL experience from an earlier project in educational leadership, facilitated this opportunity over an 8-week period in the spring of 2004. The project was made possible because of existing IP-based videoconferencing equipment in classrooms, facilitation by the Global Nomads Group (GNG) (http://www.gng.org/) and by passionate teachers and students.

Members of the GNG travel to various countries with portable satellite-based videoconferencing equipment to bring enrichment opportunities to high-school students in the United States. They made the Rwanda Alive project achievable. Students were able to interact directly with their Rwandan counterparts through GNG resources and activities. During the interactive sessions, students shared video clips, photos, and perspectives as they discussed various aspects of their respective countries and experiences.

Students in Maize, Kansas, and Kigali, Rwanda, *painted their cages* during the first session and shared a video clip featuring their district, school and personal information. In the second and third sessions they dealt with the 1994 genocide and shared perspectives on this tragic event. The third videoconference, on April 21, happened to be on the 10th anniversary of the Rwandan genocide and was broadcast directly from a site bearing traces of the genocide. This brought to the students a unique perspective on its effects at a personal level. This was a deeply emotional experience for the Maize students and cathartic for the Kigali students. During the fourth session, the HIV/AIDS epidemic and its immediate impact was shared. Session 5 introduced the students to the forgotten Ba'Twa people, a little-known indigenous population, who still depend on the rainforest for survival. In sessions 6 and 7, the students were exposed to the work of Dian Fossey and the Karisoke Research Center for the mountain gorillas of Rwanda. This included a live video feed of a family of gorillas in the wild. It was the first time that mountain gorillas had ever been observed, live, in their natural environment by a videoconference link. The students were sufficiently engaged in the process that they willingly attended the 5 A.M. session. The GNG needed to get to the Karisoke Research Center early in the day so that they could return to Kigali before nightfall. Students coreflected on what they had learned during this series of interactions in the eighth and final session.

As a follow-up to the videoconferences, the students participated in online discussions through Blackboard, and exchanged e-mails. The senior students at Maize High School were so moved by the environment and hardships of the young Rwandans, who were orphaned during the genocide that they conducted a Red Hat Day to raise funds for an orphanage in Rwanda. In 1 day, they raised over U.S.$500. This was enormous amount of money for Rwanda. As in other courses, the GL activity does, in some cases, lead to long term friendships between the participants. This project not only shed a light on this chapter of history, but it took the students and teachers to a level that helped them discover Rwanda and its people in a way they could never do through textbooks. Through GL activities, teachers had the opportunity to engage students and stimulate an interest in international events. For the Rwandan students, it was an emotional experience having people in another part of the world listen to their stories and empathize with their situation. Most people will agree that the world paid too little attention to the genocide in 1994. It was also an opportunity to practice their third language after Kinyarwandan and French. The Rwandans learned about the lives of ordinary American citizens and to contrast this with the stereotypical impressions presented by the world media, which is all too often influenced by foreign policy of the prevailing administration. The latter may have little to do with the views or beliefs of individuals living in the mid-West.

OVERVIEW OF GLOBAL LEARNING PROJECTS

GL experiences were introduced into a range of discipline areas at the undergraduate and graduate levels at a Mid-Western university from 2002 onwards (Rimmington, 2003; Rimmington, Gruba, Gordon, Gibson, &

Gibson, 2004). The case studies above are just three examples among many ways in which intercultural and GL experiences have been and can be integrated into courses or programs. How this is accomplished will depend on the discipline area, the philosophy of the institution and the preferences of the instructor or educational designer. Sometimes the nature of the design is serendipitous, a result of prior personal connections with overseas faculty or experts, research collaboration or chance visits. Each of the following examples presents different approaches, ideas, challenges and benefits.

Engineering

Three examples from Engineering are described here (Table 4.1). The first was in a department of Industrial and Manufacturing Engineering in a LEAN manufacturing course. It involved having students in multiple sites collaborate on the application of LEAN principles (Feld, 2001) to improve a production line. The production line was modeled using VRML (Virtual Reality Modeling Language) (Hartman & Wernecke, 1996), so that users can visualize its operation and the effects of changes. This was shared on the Internet. In a study of this class it was found that students learned at least as well as in distance interactions using technology as they did face-to-face (Whitman et al., 2005).

In a second example, sensors and remote digital controllers were attached to a heat exchange unit to measure temperatures, pressures and flow rates in real time as students remotely change settings such as set points or levels of resistance to flow. A screen was then designed so that students could see the data displayed graphically in real time and alter settings using screen icons such as knobs or sliders. It was designed so that students could also view the heat exchange unit with a camera-window on the same screen. This meant that students controlled the system and gathered data from experiments with the heat exchange unit. This is possible from anywhere in the world. The principle adopted here of a *remote laboratory* (Schmid, 1999) was that engineering departments around the world can share expensive equipment for student experiments so they are available 24/7 and thus enrich the learning experience of all students. When students in one time zone are asleep, other students in a different time zone can use the system remotely.

The third example involved the senior design students in a mechanical engineering program. This project is described above as a case study (Soschinske et al., 2006).

**Table 4.1. Global Learning Examples
(C = Class, T = Teacher, E = Expert, F = Faculty,
M = Mentor, S = Sponsor, RL = Remote Laboratory;
INT = Internal Facilitator, EXT = External Facilitator)**

Discipline	*Topic*	*Countries*	*Type of Collaboration*	*Facilitation Year Started*
Engineering	LEAN Manufacturing	–	C ↔ C	INT 02
	Remote Laboratories	–	C ↔ RL	INT 03
	Senior Design Project	Russia, UK, India	CT ↔ S	INT 04
Education	Leadership	Australia	C ↔ F	INT 02
	Science & Mathematics	Australia	C ↔ C	INT 02
	Gifted Education	Australia	C ↔ C	INT 03
	Cage Painting Workshops	Russia, India, Mexico	C ↔ E	INT 05
	Masters of Education	Russia	C ↔ F	INT 07
	ICCC Development Course	Germany, India, Qatar	CT ↔ M	INT 07
	TESOL	S. Korea, Vietnam	C ↔ C	INT 07
Business	International Business	Australia, Germany	C ↔ C	INT 04
	Logistics & Supply Chains	Turkey	C ↔ F	INT 04
Humanities	Women's Studies	Middle East, Nigeria, Swaziland	C ↔ F C ↔ C	INT 02
	Political Science	Canada	C ↔ C	INT 04
Fine Arts	Music	Ireland	C ↔ C, C ↔ E, E ↔ C	INT 04
Health	Nursing	Under development		
K-12	Maize School District	Rwanda, South Africa,	C ↔ C, C ↔ E	EXT 04
	Douglass School District	Japan, China, S. Korea	C ↔ C	EXT 04
	Hadley Middle School	India, Egypt, Canada, Russia, Trinidad	T/C ↔ T/C	EXT 07

Education

Initial examples of GL in education included a global forum in educational leadership, collaborative interactions between elementary science and mathematics education teacher candidates (e.g., Alagic, Gibson, &

Haack, 2002; Haack, Alagic, Gibson, Watters, & Rogers, 2003), gifted education (Rimmington & Gibson, 2004) educational leadership (Gibson, 2002; Gibson, Schiller, & Turk, 2003a, 2003b) and the use of robotics (e.g., Witherspoon, Reynolds, Alagic, & Copas, 2004), while more recent projects have involved site-based masters of education classes, online classes on ICCC (Alagic & Rimmington, 2008) development and on facilitating online learning and English as a Second or Other Language. These examples involved collaboration with different countries (Australia, Belarus, Russia, Qatar, Germany, India, South Korea, and Vietnam). In most of them, collaboration occurred among globally distributed pairs or teams. Participants of the more recent examples used the cage painting approach to prepare for global-reach-based experiences: the metaphor (chapter 1, this volume), the online CPLE simulator, and the scenario repository (chapter 2, this volume). For example, in the online ICCC course, students formed into teams, each with a global mentor (from Germany, India, or Qatar) to develop a new scenario for inclusion in the online repository. This model has been extended to a number of masters of education sites to assist participants in developing ICCC and cultural proficiency.

Business

The first example is a course in international business that is an essential part of any business curriculum. The students interacted with faculty or experts in Australia. In another course on entrepreneurship, students worked in American/German teams to explore possibilities for new or improved business opportunities. For example, a team analyzed the marketing in Europe of tea harvested in Darjeeling with a view to sell it to consumers in the United States. They made recommendations to the entrepreneur in Berlin. Wichita and Berlin student team members had the opportunity for exchanges and to collaborate online. An interesting aspect of this project was the overlay of the culture of entrepreneurship, company cultures and the cultures of Wichita and Berlin and the effects of this overlay on the interactions. Even though students from Wichita and Berlin overcame their national cultural differences, the culture of entrepreneurship dominated.

Another example, described by Mehmet B. Yildirim, Mehmet Barut, and Kemal Kilic (2004), is collaboration between business and engineering students in Wichita and at the two universities in Turkey. Students explored the fundamentals of global supply chain management. Almost every consumer product comprises components, materials, partial assembly or design that occurs in other countries. Oversight of the design and manufacturing of a product will therefore require intercultural communication, negotiation and collaboration. When incorrect preconceptions come into play, there is potential for miscommunication and misunderstandings, which translate to losses or delays. The challenge of understanding the cultural characteristics of another country can be as significant for success as the cost-savings when considering an outsourcing arrangement. It takes time to become familiar with the deeper cultural characteristics of another part of the world and this is complicated by the hybridity of culture due to migration (chapter 1, this volume).

Humanities

Two examples of GL projects in the humanities come from women's studies and from political science. GL has been introduced into several courses within the women's studies discipline, with opportunities for conversations with students, faculty and experts in the Middle East (Rimmington, Gruba, Gordon, Gibson, & Gibson, 2004), Nigeria and Swaziland. The connections to the other countries have been made using conference telephone calls or room-based videoconference equipment during overlap times (Figure 2.1). A great deal depends on the technology that is available at each location. Sometimes, the remote participant is at home rather than at the institution due to the time of day. In some cases, connections had to be made at 1 A.M. in Wichita to avoid Internet traffic jams at the other location. It was observed that foreign-born and minority students within the class became active contributors after seeing people from other cultures/places contributing using the technology. There are various explanations for this change in behavior. Sometimes local students had to stop and think about their interaction when they realized the people to whom they were talking were subject to a curfew or faced personal dangers if they venture outside. There were many instances of students becoming aware of their preconceptions about the culture of the people with whom they were interacting. For example, the students discovered that some people who are portrayed in the negative light by the media also shared the same aspirations as they do: peace, democracy, and safety for their families. This was important as the students sought to understand the perspective of the other people.

In another example, described by Caroline M. Shaw (2004), political science students had the opportunity to participate in an online role-play simulation system called *SimPlay* on postconflict nation building. Participants play roles like the minister for foreign affairs in Afghanistan, blending both a functional role and a particular *culture*. At each step in the

simulation, the characters exchange communications in an effort to negotiate a favorable outcome. The composition of role-play teams was
international with participants in Wichita, Kansas and Carleton University
in Ottawa, Canada. Not only were students dealing with playing different
roles, they brought different cultural and political perspectives to the interactions. The online role play system (Linser, 2004; Naidu, Ip, & Linser,
2000) was built in collaboration with Fablusi (http://www.fablusi.com/) company's principal, Roni Linser located in Melbourne, Australia.

Fine Arts

Visual arts, performance, and music are areas in which finished works
or techniques and approaches to creating new works can be shared if
there is sufficient bandwidth to transmit the required detail between
locations. One example of a GL project in the fine arts discipline was
the sharing insights into traditions of fiddling between Ireland and
America. Led by an Irish (Celtic) and an American (Appalachian)
master, students in both locations were able to undergo instruction in
the fingering and bowing techniques required to achieve particular
rhythms or patterns that are characteristic of regions within Ireland or
America (Langrall & Harrison, 2004). To some extent music can be
treated like a language with which to tell a story within each culture and
perhaps between cultures. Opportunities were provided for students at
both sites to perform together. Because of delays in the global
transmission, one site needed to start first and play one part of a
composition, but not hear the second site, while the second site then
played the other part of the composition in accompaniment. This could
be extended to additional sites providing earlier players could not hear
later players. Participants in such a class can expand their
understanding of how an instrument is played and how this relates to
cultural background, for a broader range of cultures that without the
benefit of global connections.

Experimental global dance performances presented some challenges.
In this case, one dancer at the remote site was displayed on a large screen
at the back of the stage, for the benefit of the audience. However, the local
dancer had to ignore this and watch other monitors at the front of the
stage to stay in synchrony. Those monitors were configured in mirror
reverse so the direction of both dancers would correspond. This seemed
more natural to the two dancers. Similar strategies were needed in relation to the music for the dance performance.

While the resolution of images and frame-rate of transmissions were becoming acceptable for music and performance, topics such as painting or sculpture remain a challenge unless there is a large amount of available bandwidth. Faculty and students in the fine arts are generally under-served in relation to access and bandwidth, since the perception of computer and network specialists is that this discipline does not have these needs. The opposite is true.

Health Professions

An example of an emerging need and application of GL is in progress in the nursing discipline. Both domestic nurses and nurses on international assignment, such as in the military, deal with other nurses and health professionals as well as patients from a variety of cultural backgrounds. One practical example is providing advice on which way to place babies in a cot or crib to prevent the likelihood of sudden-infant-death-syndrome. In some cultures a different practice is used. An advocacy or didactic approach usually meets with opposition, so nurses in this area have needed to spend time understanding the culture of the mother and the family and use other approaches to allow the mother to decide for herself what is the best practice.

K-12 Schools and Classrooms

Having contacts in other countries is a challenge in all disciplines and types of institutions. Faculty of higher education institutions tend to travel to international conferences and to collaborate internationally more than their counterparts in K-12 schools. Therefore an important part of facilitating GL opportunities for schools is providing introductions or ready-made connections. There is a variety of facilitators and directories on the Internet. For example, the GNG (http://www.gng.org/) runs programs, such as Rwanda Alive (Rimmington & Bever-Goodvin, 2005) in which schools can subscribe to a series of videoconferencing connections over a number of weeks. During these connections, students can interact with sister classes, experts, representatives of particular groups, or they can see built environments, natural landscape, fauna, or flora. During sequences of interactions students can be collaborating to produce some shared artifact, such as a video clip, musical composition, essay, report, coreflective journal, painting, design, dance, poetry, or invention. The finished artifact would be a learning outcome specific to the discipline, while the acts of communicating and collaborating required to produce this outcome result in improved ICC.

A science teacher from Hadley middle school (Wichita, Kansas) is using International Education and Resource Network (http://www.iearn.org/) to successfully integrate GL in her science classroom. This teacher found inspiration for bringing the world closer to her students while reflecting on the global citizenship challenges described in the book *Coming of Age in a Globalized World: The Next generation* (Adams & Carfagna, 2006).

The following section describes a synthesis of lessons learned from the above examples, each of which varied in their level of success. A broad set of factors and catalysts for success were identified. It is important to mention here that this book is itself the result of an effort to formalize what we learned from experiences in the above examples. This was for our own understanding and conceptualization necessary for our further work as well as more broadly for the benefit of others who wish to facilitate the development of ICCC in diverse and global contexts.

LESSONS LEARNED:
EMERGING INSTRUCTIONAL DESIGN BLUEPRINT

We consider the facilitation of Third Place transformative learning to be of central importance. Whatever we think we know might be questioned at some point in our lives and lead to a personal transformation. Alternatively, we can start from an assumption that deep cultural characteristics will be questioned in today's interconnected world and we need to be ready for such endeavors. Reexamining one of our beliefs, such as an atheistic worldview or being of a particular religion might help us understand better our culture and that of others. This would form the first step in developing a global mindset.

Facilitating the CPLE and GLE for Third Place transformative learning is dependent on many contextual factors. There are at least two interrelated layers of contextual factors to be considered, one inner and the other outer (Figure 4.3). The *outer layer* includes organizational factors and necessary infrastructure. The *inner layer*, relative to the outer layer is bound only by facilitators' imagination, creativity, and passion to go beyond traditional instructional approaches. Integration of cage painting and GL into a given curriculum is dependent on the nature of the content. We elaborate first on the context-sensitive aspect of the emerging instructional design blueprint: the inner and outer layers of contextual factors. Later, we expand our consideration to the content-sensitive aspect of the blueprint.

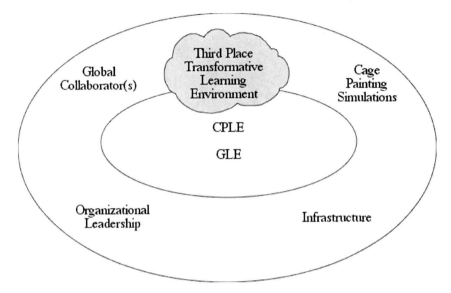

Figure 4.3. Inner and outer layers of contextual factors whose consideration appear to be essential for the instructional design blueprint, emerging from our cage painting and global learning experiences.

Context-Sensitive Aspect of the Emerging Blueprint

Inner Layer: Cage Painting and Global Learning Environments

In this section we assume ideal conditions in the outer layer, including a supportive and culturally proficient organizational leadership, necessary infrastructure, participative global collaborators, and access to CP simulations (Figure 4.3). The catalysts for occurrence of the third place transformative learning were described in earlier chapters. They include allowing all participants to have a voice through attention to power distance, encouraging critical reflection and coreflection, holistic mindfulness, shaping one's message (Enryo), and consideration of multiple perspectives (Sasshi). A period of socialization helps establish a common ground for further dialog. All these play a certain role in the resolution of an emerging or imposed preconception or disorienting dilemma (Figure 4.4).

During some of the early projects (e.g., gifted education, science & mathematics) we noticed that socialization continued throughout the semester and yielded interesting insights on preconceptions. This was due to students neither being well informed about other cultures nor having practical strategies to find answers. The pattern was one of unlearning and relearning; exploring cage painting strategies.

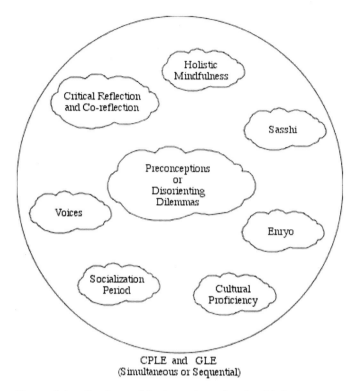

Figure 4.4.   Catalysts of the inner layer for the third place transformative learning.

Different cultures have different levels of formality between teachers and students. This reflects existing power relationships and a conduciveness to students having a voice. Inherent authority of teachers might not allow for modeling of balanced collaboration; ideally, according to authors' cultural view, the teacher becomes a colearner and models that behavior for students. In one of the projects mentioned here the teacher maintained a high power distance with his students, which affected communication of his students with a teacher from another country. Sensitivity on both sides is very important for continuing and successful collaboration.

In some disciplines (i.e., teacher preparation) *reflective practice* is nurtured more systematically than in others. Students made greater progress in understanding each others' perspectives and considering multiple perspectives when critical reflection and coreflection were facilitated as an integral part of the learning and assessment (Rimmington, O'Reilly, Gibson, & Gordon, 2003). Although holistic mindfulness was not intentionally solicited through guiding questions, our experiences and the research literature indicate that this could have a positive impact on the quality of cage painting and resolution of preconceptions (Alagic et al., 2007; Rimmington et al., 2007)

Preconceptions and disorienting dilemmas emerged in a number of projects. In earlier projects before cage painting was introduced, the approach to resolving these incongruities was ad hoc. In later projects, in which students learned cage painting strategies prior to starting, they more quickly achieved resolutions. This meant they were able to communicate and collaborate in a timely fashion. The students learned cage painting strategies with a CP simulator, which provided preconceptions or disorienting dilemmas as part of the scenarios.

Symbols and artifacts can have different meanings in different cultures. The catalysts (Figure 4.4) stimulate the transformative processes in which prior assumptions about our cultural symbols and artifacts are open to revision. During dialogic coconstruction of meaning, the reason of mindfulness takes precedence over intuition. Bhabha (1994) wrote,

> It is that Third Space, though unrepresentable in itself, which constitutes the discursive conditions of enunciation that ensure that the meaning and symbols of culture have no primordial unity or fixity; that even the same signs can be appropriated, translated, rehistoricized and read anew. (p. 55)

Outer Layer: Leadership, Infrastructure, Global Collaborators, and CP Simulations

While the above catalysts can support isolated instances of GL, success is more likely if there is support by organizational leadership, availability of infrastructure, connection with global collaborators and access to CP simulations.

Leadership

There is no doubt that adding learning outcomes of increased ICC or GL competence will help prepare graduates for an increasingly interconnected, interdependent and culturally diverse world. Institutional leaders play an important role in influencing the adoption of new practices by demonstrating a positive disposition. The leadership will be more successful in gaining shared ownership of the practices as part of the organization's vision and mission if they, themselves, exhibit high levels of ICCC (Belbin, 1993; Mant, 1997). If the leadership of the organization has a high level of cultural proficiency and they themselves participate in intercultural/global collaboration, then it is likely that other members of the organization will value and adopt such behavior. Infusion of GL into schools (e.g., the Rwanda Alive project) resulted from the enthusiasm of a leader in the district administration, who herself had gained a deeper understanding of other cultures from a GL experience in her doctoral program.

Infrastructure

In the past, access to suitable communication infrastructure has been a challenge, but more recently for most institutions in developed countries this is less of an issue. Having multiple means of global reach is becoming increasingly commonplace. Further, this is extending into some of the most remote areas of the world, using satellite-based communication. For example in the Rwanda Alive project, the GNG used portable generators and satellite antennae to operate video conferencing equipment in the middle of a wildlife park. It is in the interests of both developed and under-developed nations to improve communication infrastructure for GL.

Global Collaborators

In the projects described above (Table 4.1) there were two types of project facilitation: internal and external. Success for internally facilitated intercultural/GL depends on the existence of a globally distributed network of like-minded teachers or faculty members, who are willing to work with each other to create opportunities for their students. These collaborators deal with alignment of course syllabi, time zone differences and arrangement of semester start and end dates and public or religious holidays, compatibility of communication technologies, different learning and assessment designs and disposition of students. Most of our examples were internally facilitated (INT Table 4.1). Making use of external facilitation (EXT Table 4.1), such as that provided by iEARN or the GNG, avoids some of this complexity and overcomes lack of preexisting global connections. However, without due attention to developing internally facilitated connections, these might easily be one-time efforts in local environments.

Cage Painting Simulations

Creating the conditions for positive outcomes from intercultural or GL experiences is not simply a matter of putting people of different cultures in contact with each other using technology. For the learners to make progress, a conceptual framework is needed. The cage painting metaphor, serves as a conceptual framework that people find helpful for understanding a systematic approach to improving ICC. The transfer distance (see chapter 2, this volume) from the abstraction of a conceptual framework to its application in real situations can be bridged with a tool for practicing and refining ICCC. The cage painting simulator within the CP learning environment is such a tool. It enables the learner to develop strategies for improving his/her intercultural/global communication competences. For example, a participant in the ICCC case study above reported about successfully using the cage painting strategies in her communication with global partners as she facilitates GL activities in her school.

Content-Sensitive Aspect of the Emerging Blueprint

Traditionally, ICC classes are done in isolation from other content classes (Chen & Starosta, 2005) and this is called the *classroom model* for ICC. It suffers from disparity between the learning context and the target context of lived intercultural interactions. In the classroom model, learners may become knowledgeable *about* another culture, but are not able to learn experientially how to behave and adapt in a new culture. Two ways of taking the learning situation closer to a lived intercultural experience are through simulation or GL, which are topics of this book. Simulation may take the form of a computer game or the form of role-plays. GL involves interaction between globally distributed participants using modern communication technologies (global reach).

Simulations put the learner closer to the lived intercultural/diverse experience and can serve as preparation for GL or interactions in which the culturally diverse participants are physically copresent. The approach being suggested in this book is to integrate GL for ICCC development into discipline classes in such a way that the means to learn the discipline content is provided by GL. This may require a fresh approach to instructional design by the discipline specialist. As demonstrated above, there are many examples of such designs. The simplest may be for students to write a paper about a topic that requires them to interact with an expert in another country as in the Women's Studies example. A more complex example is for student teams with globally distributed, culturally diverse members to work on a project for a sponsor of yet another culture, as in the mechanical engineering case study (p. 116, this volume).

The reason we say a *fresh* approach may be needed is that outside the discipline of education, such learning processes as critical reflection and coreflection, metacognitive apprenticeship or dialectic thinking, may be unknown. In such cases redesign of learning will require a team comprising the discipline specialist, an educational designer and an ICC specialist. In the examples and case studies above, the more successful projects outside of education did involve such teams. In those cases where a GL or

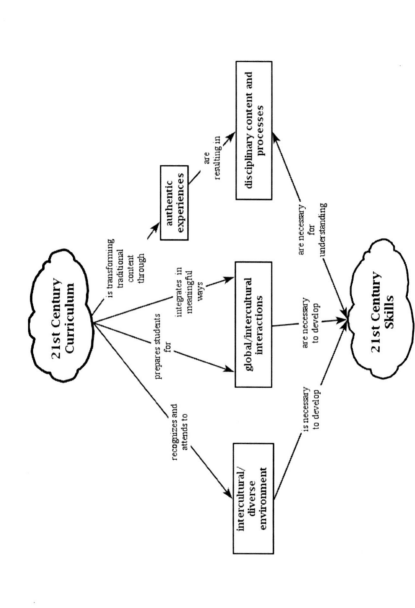

Figure 4.5.　Authentic learning in the twenty-first century.

intercultural interaction was simply added on top of other activities and were not assessed, such activities did not persist.

In an ideal situation, a new curriculum for the twenty-first century (Figure 4.5) will incorporate global/intercultural interactions into authentic project-based learning as the means by which learning of discipline content occurs. The additional outcome of ICCC development will be assessed along with learning outcomes that are discipline related. The learning will necessarily be social in nature so as to require collaboration between learners of different cultures. An associated benefit of this new curriculum will be increased authenticity within the discipline area. In addition, the participants become familiar with and practiced in being active members of a learning community, possibly on a global scale. Emergent instructional design that incorporates integrated formative evaluation for continuous improvement will be needed to be able to adapt to new contexts and combinations of cultures.

> There is no way to know beforehand for every site what will resonate and what local concerns and local knowledge exist. What one can assume is that there always is something. Using the Emergent Design framework, combined with principles of learning environments and open, programmable, technological tools, this "something" can be built upon and leveraged. (Cavallo, 2000, p. 781)

SUMMARY: WHERE WE ARE AND WHERE WE ARE GOING?

GL represents a concrete example of a context in which facilitating learning processes might lead to third place transformative learning. Using the cage painting simulator strengthens those processes by providing appropriate simulated experiences. Ideally, the GLE is designed as a metacognitive apprenticeship in which learners are guided through the processes of understanding and applying cage painting to overcome preconceptions or disorienting dilemmas. Some case studies and examples of attempts to integrate GL into courses have been presented. They varied in success. Reflection on this suite of examples led to the emergence of an instructional design blueprint for GLEs in which transformative third place learning might occur. Similarly, it can be applied to the multicultural classroom. Critical conditions or catalysts for success were identified. These can serve as signposts for those who wish to facilitate third place learning processes for both contexts: GL, in which participants are distributed around the world, connected using communication technologies; and classrooms with physically copresent students of multicultural backgrounds.

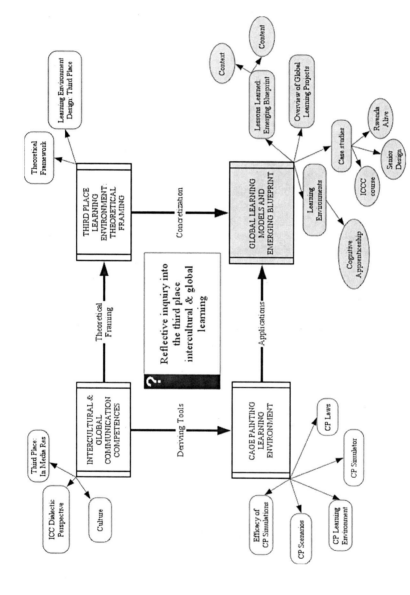

Figure 4.6.   An emerging instructional design blueprint for the third place intercultural and global learning.

CHAPTER 5

CONCLUSION

Further Reflective Inquiry
Into Third Place Learning

Come to the edge the voice said softly
No they said it's too high
Come to the edge the voice insisted
No she said it's too dangerous
Come to the edge the voice demanded
No he said I might fall
Come to the edge the voice commanded
Reluctantly, I came to the edge
He pushed me off
And I flew.
—Guillaume Apollinaire, 1870-1918

Our goal in this short chapter is to engage the reader in further reflective inquiry into third learning. Our first consideration is to our own reflective inquiry path from global learning projects to third place learning, guided by two questions: How practice informs theory? and How theory informs practice? This leads to deliberation on the contribution of these ideas to the knowledge basis for diversity (Huber-Warring, Mitchell, Alagic, & Gibson. 2005; Smith, 1998).

Third Place Learning: Reflective Inquiry Into Intercultural and Global Cage Painting
pp. 135–139

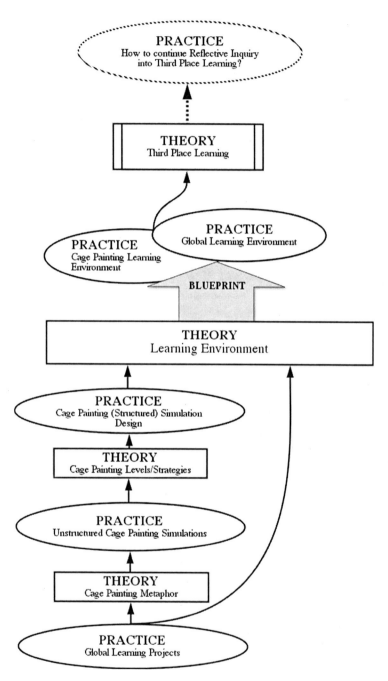

Figure 5.1.   Reflective inquiry into Third Place Learning: Interplay of theory and practice.

REFLECTIVE INQUIRY INTO THE THIRD PLACE LEARNING: INTERPLAY OF THEORY AND PRACTICE

Our understanding of the reflective inquiry, as captured by this book, has evolved according to interplay between *theory* and *practice, practice* and *theory* as represented in Figure 5.1 opposite page. The following section provides a very brief summary of this evolution.

Global Learning Projects => Cage Painting Metaphor

Reflecting on the initial global learning projects, we realized that intercultural communication, particularly contextualized listening, was both a challenge and an inspiration for developing a conceptual framework. This was achieved by extending the cage metaphor of Hugh Mackay (1994) to our cage painting metaphor (chapter 1, this volume).

Cage Painting Theory => Unstructured Cage Painting Simulations

To implement the cage painting idea in a way that would assist learners to improve their intercultural communication, we designed an appropriate computer simulation. Cage painting simulations at this point revolved around miscommunication examples and did not have a formal underlying structure. Simulations were embedded in a learning activity that began and finished with guided reflections.

Unstructured Cage Painting Simulations => Cage Painting Levels/Strategies

During our efforts to make simulations more accessible via Internet and provide broader range of contexts, we realized that an underlying structure was needed. From the educational point of view, we also wanted to complete the learning cycle (Figure 2.10) by having learners apply what they learned to the design of new simulation scenarios. This lead to a qualitative change, conceptualized theoretically through four cage painting levels (chapter 2, this volume, Figure 2.5).

Cage Painting Levels/Strategies => Cage Painting (Structured) Simulation Design

Having derived a discrete number of cage painting levels we were able to create a template for authoring scenarios. Learners now have an opportunity to design scenarios from which simulations can be generated and stored in a Web 2.0 repository. Furthermore, simulations are clustered according to the contexts in which they can be applied: education, business.

Cage Painting (Structured) Simulation Design and Global Learning Projects => Learning Environment

A learning environment that encapsulates cage painting and global learning processes was framed within a cognitive apprenticeship methodology (Figures 3.7a-d). Cage painting and global learning are incorporated in this learning environment model in either sequential or simultaneous fashion. From the interplay of the cage painting learning environment (CPLE) and global learning environment (GLE) processes (Figure 4.2) *emerged a blueprint* for integrating cage painting and global learning opportunities into a curriculum.

CPLE and GLE Blueprint => CPLE and GLE in Practice

The ICCC Development course, described in chapter 4, represents an example of this blueprint's implementation, although not in its entirety, because it was condensed into an 8-week course and because not all elements of the blueprint had yet emerged. In fact some elements described in this book were the result of reflective inquiry during and after that course. Attention was paid to the contextual aspects of learning environment as portrayed in Figure 4.3 and to some of the catalysts for the Third Place transformative learning (Figure 4.4).

CPLE and GLE in Practice => Third Place Learning

The pivotal point of our reflective inquiry is our own conceptualization of Third Place Learning that brought together many different paths toward intercultural communication development (In Media Res, chapter 1, this volume; and Systems View, chapter 3, this volume). It came about as we realized that the essential ingredient for successful cage painting or global learning was facilitating Third Place Processes for transformative learning (Figures 4.3 and 4.4).

Third Place Processes => How to Continue Reflective Inquiry Into Third Place Learning

The Third Place Learning can be facilitated by (1) encouraging a socialization phase, (2) cultivation of Enryo-Sasshi and multiple perspectives; (3) dialectic thinking; (4) cognizance of power distance; (5) ensuring everyone has a voice; (6) introducing a disorienting dilemma to take the participants to the edge; (7) cultivating holistic mindfulness; and (8) encouraging critical reflection through guiding questions. Hence, it appears that theoretical framing of Third Place Learning is specific enough for implementation in practice. However, the abstractness of the *Third Place* continues to challenge our thinking. Deeper understanding of the Third Place is an ongoing quest. What questions do you (teacher, professional developer, student, manager, engineer, human resources leader) need to ask and explore? Continuing reflective inquiry into theory and practice of the Third Place processes promises further contribution to the knowledge bases for intercultural communication in culturally diverse environments, both local and global.

REFERENCES

Adams, J. Michael, & Angelo Carfagna. (2006). *Coming of age in a globalized world: The next generation*. Bloomfield, CT: Kumarian Press.

Alagic, Mara, Kay L. Gibson, & Connie Haack. (2002). Learning to teach elementary mathematics and science: A global learning dimension. *Proceedings of the International Conference on Computers in Education (ICCE 2002), Auckland, New Zealand*. pp. 1037-1038 [Online]. Retrieved June 2006, from http://csdl2.computer.org/persagen/DLAbsToc.jsp?resourcePath=/dl/proceedings/&toc=comp/proceedings/icce/2002/1509/00/1509toc.xml

Alagic, Mara, Kay L. Gibson, & Glyn M. Rimmington. (2007). Co-constructing intercultural communication competence through an online cage painting simulation and scenario repository: A theoretical perspective. In Sankaran Manikutty (Ed.), *Learning, teaching and research in a borderless world.* (pp. 118-150). New Delhi, India: Macmillan.

Alagic, Mara, & Glyn M. Rimmington. (2008, , March 24-28). *The Cage Painting Simulator Implementation: A case study*. Paper presented at the American Educational Research Association (AERA), New York.

Alagic, Mara, Catherine Yeotis, Glyn M. Rimmington, & David N. Koert. (2003). Inquiry and information technology integration: Cognitive apprenticeship learning environment model (CALEM). *Proceedings of the SITE 2003 14th International Conference of the Society for Information Technology & Teacher Education. Association for Advancement of Computers in Education, Albuquerque, NM*, 826-833.

Antal, Ariane Berthoin, & Victor Friedman. (2003). Negotiating reality as an approach to intercultural competence [Electronic Version]. *Journal*. Retrieved July 2007, from http://skylla.wz-berlin.de/pdf/2003/iii03-101.pdf

Appiah, Kwame Anthony. (2006). *Cosmopolitanism: Ethics in a world of strangers*. New York: W. W. Norton.

Apps, Jerold W. (1991). *Mastering the teaching of adults*. Malabar, FL: Krieger.

Argyris, Chris. (1999). *On organizational learning* (2nd ed.). Malden, MA: Blackwell.

Bakhtin, Mikhail Milhailovich. (1984). *Problems of Dostoevsky's poetics.* (Caryl Emerson, Trans.). Minneapolis, MN: University of Minnesota Press. (Original work published 1929)

Bandura, Albert. (1986). *Social foundations of thought and action: A social cognitive theory.* Englewood Cliffs, NJ: Prentice Hall.

Banks, James A. (Ed.). (1996). *Multicultural education, transformative knowledge, & action: Historical and contemporary perspectives.* Columbia, NY: Teachers College Press.

Banks, James A. (2006). *Race, culture, and education: The selected works of James A. Banks.* New York: Routledge.

Bannan-Ritland, Brenda, Nada Dabbagh, & Kate Murphy. (2002). Learning object systems as constructivist learning environments: Related assumptions, theories and applications. In D. A. Wiley (Ed.), *The instructional use of learning objects* (pp. 61-98). Bloomington, Indiana: AIT/AECT [Online] Retrieved June 2006, from http://reusability.org/read/Chapters/bannan-ritland.doc

Barab, Sasha A., & Thomas M. Duffy. (2000). From practice fields to communities of practice In David H. Jonassen & Susan Land (Eds.), *Theoretical foundations of learning environments* (pp. 25-56). Mahwah, NJ: Erlbaum.

Barnlund, Dean C. (1988). Communication in a global village. In Larry A. Samovar & Richard E. Porter (Eds.), *Intercultural communication: A reader.* Belmont, CA: Wadsworth.

Basseches, Michael. (1980). Dialectic schemata: A framework for the empirical study of the development of dialectic thinking. *Human Development, 23,* 400-421.

Basseches, Michael. (1984). *Dialectical thinking and adult development* (1st ed.). Norwood, NJ: Ablex.

Bednar, Anne K., David Cunningham, Thomas M. Duffy & David J. Perry. (1992). Theory into practice: How do we link? In Thomas M. Duffy & David H. Jonassen (Eds.), *Constructivism and the technology of instruction: A conversation* (pp. 17-35). Hillsdale, NJ: Erlbaum.

Belbin, R. Meredith. (1993). *Team roles at work.* Oxford, England: Butterworth-Heinemann.

Bell, Maureen. (2001). A case study of an online role play for academic Staff. In Gregor Kennedy, Mike Keppell, Carmel McNaught & Tom Petrovic (Eds.), *Meeting at the Crossroads, 18th Annual Conference of the Australasian Society for Computers in Learning in Tertiary Education* (pp. 63-72). Melbourne: Australasian Society for Computers in Learning in Tertiary Education.

Bennett, Christine I. (1990). *Comprehensive multicultural education: Theory and practice* (2nd ed.). Boston: Allyn & Bacon.

Bennett, Milton J. (1986). A developmental approach to training for intercultural sensitivity. *International Journal of Intercultural Relations, 10*(2), 179-195.

Bennett, Milton J. (1993). Towards ethnorelativism: A developmental model of intercultural sensitivity. In R. Michael Paige (Ed.), *Education for the intercultural experience* (pp. 21-71). Yarmouth, ME: Intercultural Press.

Berry, John W., Ype H. Poortinga, Marshall H. Segall, & Pierre R. Dasen. (2002). *Cross-cultural psychology: Research and applications* (2nd ed.). Cambridge, England: Cambridge University Press.

Bertalanffy, Ludwig von. (1968). *General systems theory: Foundations, developments, applications.* New York: Braziller.

Bhabha, Homi K. (1994). *The location of culture* (Routledge Classics Edition). New York: Routledge.

Bhattacharya, Kalidas. (1977). *On the concepts of relation and negation in Indian philosophy.* Calcutta, India: Sanskrit College.

Bogdan, Robert C., & Sari Knopp Biklen. (2003). *Qualitative research for education: An introduction to theorists and methods* (4th ed.). Boston: Pearson Education Group.

Boulding, Kenneth E. (1985). *The world as a total system.* Newbury Park, CA: SAGE.

Boyd, Robert D., & J. Gordon Myers. (1988). Transformative education. *International Journal of Lifelong Education, 7*(4), 261-284.

Bretag, Tracey. (2006). Developing "third space" intercultural using computer-mediated communication. *Journal, 11*(4). Retrieved September 2007, from http://jcmc.indiana.edu/vol11/issue4/betag.html

Brown, John Seely, Allan Collins, & Paul Duguid. (1989). Situated cognition and the culture of learning. *Educational Researcher, 18*, 32-42.

Bruner, Jerome Seymour. (1990). *Acts of meaning.* Cambridge, MA: Harvard University Press.

Bruner, Jerome Seymour. (1984). Vygotsky's zone of proximal development: The hidden agenda. In Barbara Rogoff & James V. Wertsch (Eds.), *Children's learning in the "zone of proximal development"* (pp. 93-97). San Francisco: Jossey-Bass.

Burgoon, Judee K., Charles R. Berger, & Vincent R. Waldron. (2000). Mindfulness and interpersonal communication. *Journal of Social Issues, 56*(1), 105-127.

Burns, David D. (1980). *Feeling good: The new mood therapy.* New York: William Morrow.

Burrell, Gibson, & Gareth Morgan. (1988). *Sociological paradigms and organizational analysis.* Portsmouth, NH: Heinemann.

Cavallo, David Paul. (2000). Emergent design and learning environments: Building on indigenous knowledge *Journal, 39*(3 & 4). Retrieved July 2007, from http://www.research.ibm.com/journal/sj/393/part2/cavallo.html

Chen, Guo-Ming. (1989). Relationships of the dimensions of intercultural communication competence. *Communication Quarterly, 37*, 118-133.

Chen, Guo-Ming. (2005). A model of global communication competence. *China Media Research, 1*(1), 3-11.

Chen, Guo-Ming, & William J. Starosta. (2004). Communication among cultural diversities: A dialogue. *International and Intercultural Communication Annual, 27*, 3-16.

Chen, Guo-Ming, & William J. Starosta. (2005). *Foundations of intercultural communication.* Lanham, MD: University Press of America.

Chester, Andrea, & Gillian Gwynne. (1998). Online Teaching: Encouraging collaboration through anonymity. *Journal of Computer-Mediated*

Communication's 4(2). Retrieved August 2007, from http://jcmc.indiana.edu/ vol4/issue2/chester.html

Clarke, Richard L. W. (2000). Root versus rhizome: An "epistemological break" in (Francophone) Caribbean thought? *Journal of West Indian Literature, 9*(1), 12-41.

Cobb, Paul. (1994). Where is the mind? Constructivist and sociocultural perspectives on mathematical development. *Educational Researcher, 23*(7), 13-20.

Collier, Mary Jane. (1991). Conflict competence within African, Mexican and Anglo American Friendships. In Stella Ting-Toomey & Felipe Korzenny (Eds.), *Cross-cultural interpersonal communication* (pp. 132-154). Newbury Park, CA: SAGE.

Collier, Mary Jane. (2005). Theorizing cultural identifications: Critical updates and continuing evolution. In William B. Gudykunst (Ed.), *Theorizing about intercultural communication* (pp. 235-256). Thousand Oaks, CA: SAGE.

Collins, Allan. (1991). Cognitive apprenticeship and instructional technology. In Lorna Idol & Beau Fly Jones (Eds.), *Educational values and cognitive instruction: Implications for reform* (pp. 121-138). Hillsdale, NJ: Erlbaum.

Collins, Allan, John Seely Brown, & Susan E. Newman. (1989). Cognitive apprenticeship: Teaching the crafts of reading, writing, and mathematics. In Lauren B. Resnick (Ed.), *Knowing, learning, and instruction: Essays in honor of Robert Glaser* (pp. 453-494). Hillsdale, NJ: Erlbaum.

Crotty, Michael. (2003). *The foundations of social research: Meaning and perspective in the research process.* Thousand Oaks, CA: SAGE.

Deleuze, Gilles, Felix Guattari, & Brian Massumi. (1988). *A thousand plateaus: Capitalism and schizophrenia.* London: Athlone Press.

Denzin, Norman K., & Yvonna S. Lincoln. (Eds.). (2005). *The SAGE handbook of qualitative research* (3rd ed.). Thousand Oaks, CA: SAGE.

Derry, Sharon J. (1990). Learning strategies for acquiring useful knowledge. In Beau Fly Jones & Lorna Idol (Eds.), *Dimensions of thinking and cognitive instruction* (pp. 347-379). Hillsdale, NJ: Erlbaum.

Detweiler, R. A. (1975). On inferring the intentions of a person from another culture. *Journal of Personality, 43*(4), 591-611.

Dewey, John. (1933). *How we think: A restatement of the relation of reflective thinking to the educative process* (1st ed.). Boston: D.C. Heath. (Original work published 1910)

Dewey, John. (1944). *Democracy and education.* New York: Free Press.

Dodd, Carley H. (1998). *Dynamics of intercultural communication.* Boston: McGraw-Hill.

Edmundson, Andrea. (2007). The cultural adaptation process (CAP) model: Designing e-learning for another culture. In Andrea Edmundson (Ed.), *Globalized e-learning cultural challenges* (pp. 267-291). Hershey, PA: Information Science.

Elmer, Muriel I. (1986). *Intercultural effectiveness: Development of an intercultural competency scale.* East Lansing: Michigan State University.

Feld, William M. (2001). *Lean Manufacturing: Tools, techniques, and how to use them.* Boca Raton, FL: CRC Press.

Flavell, John H. (1979). Metacognition and cognitive monitoring: A new area of cognitive developmental inquiry *American Psychologist, 34,* 906-911.

Fox, Frampton F. (2003). Reducing intercultural friction through fiction: Virtual cultural learning. *International Journal of International Relations, 27,* 99-123.

Freeman, Mark A., & John M. Capper. (1999). Exploiting the web for education: an anonymous asynchronous role simulation. *Australian Journal of Educational Technology, 15*(1), 95-116.

Freire, Paulo. ([1968]1993). *Pedagogy of the oppressed* (Myra Bergman Ramos, Trans.). London and New York: Penguin.

Friedman, Thomas L. (2005). *The world is flat: A brief history of the twenty-first century.* New York: Farrar, Straus and Giroux.

Foucault, M. (1980). *Power/knowledge.* New York: Pantheon.

Gadamer, Hans-George. (1981). *Reason in the age of science* (Frederick G. Lawrence, Trans.). Cambridge, MA: MIT Press.

Gadamer, Hans-George. (1987). The problem of historical consciousness. In Paul Rabinow & William M. Sullivan (Eds.), *Interpretive social science* (pp. 82-140). Berkeley, CA: University of California Press.

Gannon, Martin J. (2001). *Cultural metaphors: Readings, research translations, and commentary.* Thousand Oaks, CA: SAGE.

Gibson, Ian W. (2002, June 24-29). Developing a global forum on school leadership: Using interactive communications technology to enhance the achievement of learning goals in a school leader preparation program. *Proceedings of the Ed-Media 2002 World conference on educational multimedia, hypermedia & telecommunications. Association for the Advancement of Computing in Education, Denver, CO,* 612-613.

Gibson, Ian W., John Schiller, & Randy Turk. (2003a, March 24-29). A global online forum for educational leadership. *Proceedings of the SITE 2003 14th International Conference of the Society for Information Technology & Teacher Education, Albuquerque, NM,* 1289-1292.

Gibson, Ian W., John Schiller, & Randy Turk. (2003b, June 23-28). Evaluating the quality of global learning experiences: Considering the interplay between interactive technology and assessment on an international learning community. *Proceedings of the EdMedia 2003. World conference on educational multimedia, hypermedia & telecommunications. Association for the Advancement of Computing in Education, Honolulu, HI,* 3093-3096.

Giroux, Henry A. (1992). *Border crossing: Cultural workers and the politics of education.* London: Routledge.

Giroux, Henry A. (1995). The politics of insurgent multiculturalism in the era of the Los Angeles uprising. In Barry Kanpol & Peter McLaren (Eds.), *Critical multiculturalism: Uncommon voices in a common struggle* (pp. 107-124). Westport, CT: Bergin & Gravey.

Giroux, Henry A. (2003). Critical theory and educational practice. In Aantonia Darder, Marta Baltodano & Rudelpho D. Torres (Eds.), *The critical pedagogy reader.* (pp. 27-56). New York: Routledge Farmer.

Grant, Carl A., & Gloria Ladson-Billings. (Eds.). (1997). *Dictionary of multicultural education.* Phoenix, AZ: The Oryx Press.

Greeno, James G. (1989). A perspective on thinking. *American Psychologist, 44*, 134-141.

Gudykunst, William B. (1998). *Bridging differences: Effective intergroup communication* (3rd ed.). Thousand Oaks, CA: Sage Publications.

Gudykunst, William B. (Ed.). (2005). *Theorizing about intercultural communication*. Thousand Oaks, CA: SAGE.

Gudykunst, William B., Mitchell R. Hammer, & Richard L. Wiseman. (1977). An analysis of an integrated approach to cross-cultural training. *International journal of intercultural relations, 8*, 1-10.

Haack, Connie, Mara Alagic, Kay Gibson, James J. Watters, & A. Geoff. Rogers. (2003). Tailoring a website to meet the needs of global learners. *Proceedings of the International Society for Information Technology & Teacher Education International Conference (SITE 2003). Albuquerque, NM*, 2396-2399.

Hall, Edward Twitchell. (1959). *The silent language*. Garden City, NY: Doubleday.

Hall, Edward Twitchell. (1966). *The hidden dimension*. Garden City, NY: Doubleday.

Hall, Edward Twitchell. (1977). *Beyond culture*. Garden City, NY: Anchor Press.

Hall, Stuart. (1993). Cultural identity and diaspora. In Patrick Williams & Laura Chrisman (Eds.), *Colonial discourse and post-colonial theory* (pp. 392-403). New York: Harvester Wheatsheaf.

Hannafin, Michael, Susan Land, & Ron Oliver. (1999). Open learning environments: Foundations, methods, and models. In Charles M. Reigeluth (Ed.), *Instructional design theories and models: A new paradigm of instructional theory* (Vol. 2, pp. 115-140). Mahwah, NJ: Erlbaum.

Harasim, Linda, Stan Roxanne Hiltz, Lucio Teles, & Murray Turoff. (1995). *Learning networks: A field guide to teaching and learning online*. Cambridge, MA: MIT Press.

Hartman, Joel, Patsy Moskal, & Chuck Dziuban. (2006). Preparing the academy of today for the learner of tomorrow [Electronic source]. Retrieved June 2006, from http://www.educause.edu/content.asp?page_id=6062&bhcp=1

Hartman, Joel, & Josie Wernecke. (1996). *The VRML 2.0 handbook: Building moving worlds on the web*. Redwood City, CA: Addison Wesley Longman.

Herman, Andrew, Rosemary J. Coombe, & Lewis Kaye. (2006). Your second life? *Cultural Studies, 20*(2), 184-210.

Herrington, Jan, & Ron Oliver. (1995). Critical characteristics of situated learning: Implications for the instructional design of multimedia. In Jon Pearce & Allan Ellis (Eds.), *ASCILITE95 Conference Proceedings* (pp. 253-262). Melbourne, Australia: University of Melbourne.

Hodge, Sheida. (2000). *Global smarts. The art of communicating and deal making anywhere in the world*. New York: John Wiley.

Hofstede, Geert. (1980). Motivation, leadership and organization: do American theories apply abroad? *Organisational Dynamics, 9*(1), 42-63.

Hofstede, Geert. (1991). *Cultures and organizations: Software of the mind*. New York: McGraw Hill.

Huber-Warring, Tonya, Lynda Mitchell, Mara Alagic, & Ian Gibson. (2005). Multicultural/diversity outcomes: Assessing students' knowledge bases across programs in one college of education. *Journal of Thought, 40*(3), 25-50.

Ishii, Satoshi. (1984). Enryo-sasshi communication: A key to understanding Japanese interpersonal relations. *Cross Currents, 11*(1), 49-58.

Jensen, Iben. (2003). The practice of intercultural communication: Reflections for professionals in cultural meetings. *Journal of Intercultural Communication, 6.* Retrieved November 21, 2007, from http://www.immi.se/intercultural/

Jonassen, David H., & Thomas Charles Reeves. (1996). Learning with technology: Using computers as cognitive tools. In David H. Jonassen (Ed.), *Handbook of research for educational communications and technology* (pp. 693-719). New York: Macmillan.

Karplus, Robert, & Herbert Their. (1967). *A new look at elementary school science.* Chicago: Rand McNally.

Kealey, Daniel J. (2000). *Cross-cultural effectiveness: A study of Canadian technical advisors overseas.* Retrieved November 21, 2007, from http://publications.gc.ca

Kim, Yun Young. (1988). *Communication and cross-cultural adaptation.* Clevedon, England: Multilingual Matters.

Kim, Yun Young. (1994). Beyond cultural identity. *Intercultural Communication Studies, 4*(1), 1-24.

Kincheloe, Joe L., & Steinberg, S. R. (1997). *Changing multiculturalism.* Bristol, PA: Open University Press.

Kincheloe, Joe L. (2005). *Critical pedagogy.* New York: Peter Lang.

Kitchener, Karen. (1983). Cognition, metacognition and epistemic cognition. *Human Development, 26*(4), 222-223.

Kluckhohn, Florence Rockwood, & Fred L. Strodtbeck. (1961). *Variations in value orientations.* Evanston, IL: Row, Peterson.

Kolb, David A. (1984). *Experiential learning.* Englewood Cliffs, NJ: Prentice Hall.

Kolb, David A., & Roger Fry. (1975). Toward an applied theory of experiential learning. In Catherine R. Cooper (Ed.), *Theories of group process* (pp. 33-58). London: Wiley.

Kosok, Michael. (1972). The formalization of Hegel's dialectical logic: Its formal structure, logical interpretation and intuitive foundation. In Alasdair C. MacIntyre (Ed.), *Hegel: A collection of critical essays* (pp. 237-287). London: University of Notre Dame Press.

Laertius, Diogenes. (2000). *Lives of Eminent Philosophers* (R. D. Hicks, Trans.). Cambridge, MA: Harvard University Press. (Original work published 1925)

Lakoff, George, & Mark Johnson. (1980). *Metaphors we live by.* Chicago: University of Chicago.

Lam, Wan Shun Eva. (2006). Culture and Learning in the context of Globalization: Research Directions. In Judith Green & Allan Luke (Eds.), *Rethinking Learning: What counts as Learning and What Learning Counts. Review of Research in Education* (pp. 213-237). Washington, DC: American Educational Research Association.

Lampert, Magdalene. (1990). When the problem is not the question and the solution is not the answer: Mathematical knowing and teaching. *American Educational Research Journal, 27,* 29-63.

Langer, Ellen J. (1997). *The power of mindful learning.* Reading, MA: Addison-Wesley.

Langer, Ellen J. (1989). *Mindfulness.* Reading, MA: Addison-Wesley.

Langrall, Rebecca, & John Harrison. (2004). Sharing music, sharing culture: Using Internet2 and Blackboard to explore Ireland and the US through string improvisation. *Proceedings of the 15th International Conference of the Society for Information Technology & Teacher Education. Association for Advancement of Computers in Education (SITE 2004), Atlanta, GA.*

Lave, Jean, & Etienne Wenger. (1991). *Situated learning: Legitimate peripheral participation.* New York: Cambridge University Press.

Lawson, Anton E., Michael R. Abraham, & John Wilson Renner (1989). *A theory of instruction: Using the learning cycle to teach science concepts and thinking skills [Monograph, Number One].* Manhattan, KS: National Association for Research in Science Teaching.

Lemire, Daniel (2006). Death of learning objects [Electronic version]. Retrieved June 26, 2006, from http://www.daniel-lemire.com/blog/archives/2006/01/09/death-of-learning-objects/

Lewis, Tom J, & Robert E. Jungman (1986). *On being foreign: Culture shock in short fiction.* Yarmouth: Intercultural Press.

Liddicoat, Anthony J. (2002). Static and dynamic views of culture and intercultural language acquisition. *Babel, 36*(3), 4-11.

Lindner, Evelin G. (2006a). *Avoiding humiliation—From intercultural communication to global interhuman communication.* Lecture at the Society for Intercultural Education, Training and Research (SIETAR) Japan, Reitaku University Tokyo. Retrieved from http://www.humiliationstudies.org/documents/evelin/AvoidingHumiliationSIETAR06.pdf

Lindner, Evelin G. (2006b). *Making enemies unwittingly: Humiliation and international conflict.* Westport, CT: Praeger.

Lindsey, Randall B., Kikanza Nuri Robins & Raymond D. Terrell. (2003). *Cultural proficiency: A manual for school leaders.* Thousand Oaks, CA: Corwin Press.

Linser, Roni. (2004). Suppose you were someone else: The learning environment of a web-based role-play simulation. *Proceedings of the 15th International Conference of the Society for Information Technology & Teacher Education. Association for Advancement of Computers in Education (SITE 2004), Atlanta, GA,* 2403-2408.

Lionni, Leo. (1970). *Fish is fish.* New York: Dragonfly Books, Alfred A. Knopf.

Lucas, Louis L. (1994). The role of courage in transformative learning (Doctoral dissertation, University of Wisconsin-Madison, 1994). *Dissertation Abstracts International, 56*(01A), 60.

Lucena, Juan C. (2002). Being political in the global: How engineers accommodate, resist and experience ambiguity towards globalization (CD). *Proceedings of the 2002 ASEE Annual Conference and Exposition. Vive L'ingenieur! Montreal, Canada.*

Mackay, Hugh (1994). *Why don't people listen? Solving the communication problem.* Sydney: Pan.

Mant, Alistair. (1997). *Intelligent leadership.* St Leonards, NSW Australia: Allen & Unwin.

Martin, Judith N., & Thomas K Nakayama. (1999). Thinking dialectically about culture and communication. *Communication Theory, 9*(1), 1-25.

McCoy, Scott. (2003, August). *Integrating national culture into individual IS adoption research: The need for individual level measures.* Paper presented at the 9th Americas' Conference on Information Systems (AMCIS), Tampa, FL.

McLoughlin, Catherine. (2002). Learner support in distance and networked learning environments: Ten dimensions for successful design. *Distance Education, 23*(2), 149-162.

McSweeney, Brendan. (2002). Hofstede's model of national cultural differences and their consequences" a triumph of faith—a failure of analysis. *Human relations, 55(1)*, 89-118.

Mead, Margaret. (1928). *Coming of age in Samoa: A psychological study of primitive youth for western civilization.* New York: Morrow.

Merriam, Sharon B. (1998). *Qualitative research and case study applications in education.* San Francisco: Jossey-Bass.

Meyer, John W. (2002). Globalization and the expansion and Standardization of Management. In Lars Engwall & Kerstin Sahlin-Andersson (Eds.), *Management knowledge: Carriers and Circulation* (pp. 33-43). Hamburg, Germany: Gesellschaft fur Arbeit, Technik und Entwicklung.

Mezirow, Jack. (1991). *Transformative dimensions of adult learning.* San Francisco, CA: Jossey-Bass.

Mezirow, Jack. (1998). On critical reflection. *Adult Education Quarterly, 48*(3), 185-198.

Mezirow, Jack. (Ed.). (2000). *Learning as transformation: Critical perspectives on a theory in progress.* San Francisco, CA: Jossey-Bass.

Mindell, Arnold. (1990). *Working on yourself alone: Inner dreambody work.* London: Arkana.

Mishra, Vijay. (2005). What is multiculturalism? *Portal Journey of Multidisciplinary Studies, 2*(2), 2-47.

Moss, Pamela A., Brian J. Girard, & Laura C. Haniford. (2006). Validity in educational assessment. In Judith Green & Allan Luke (Eds.), *Rethinking learning: What counts as learning and what learning counts* (pp. 109-162). Washington, DC: American Educational Research Association.

Murchison, Carl Allanmore. (Ed.). (1973). *Psychology of 1930.* New York: Arno Press.

Nagata, Adair Linn. (2003). Mindful inquiry: A learner-centered approach to qualitative research. *Journal of Intercultural Communication, 6*, 23-36.

Nagata, Adair Linn. (2006). Transformative learning in intercultural education. *Rikkyo Intercultural Communication Review, 4*, 39-60.

Nagata, Adair Linn. (2007). Bodymindfulness for skillful communication. *Rikkyo Intercultural Communication Review, 5*, 61-76.

Naidu, Som, Albert Ip, & Roni Linser. (2000). Dynamic Goal-Based Role-Play Simulation on the Web: A Case Study. *Educational Technology & Society, 3*(3), 190-202.

National Research Council. (2000). *How people learn: Brain, mind, experience, and school: Expanded edition.* Washington, DC: National Academy Press.

Novak, George. (pseudonym: Ward, Wm.F) (1940). Engel's dialectics of nature. *Fourth International, 1*(7), 201-205. Retrieved May 1, 2008, from http://www.marxists.org/archive/novack/1940/12/dialnat.htm

Nieto, Sonia. (1999). Critical multicultural education and students' perspectives. In Stephen May (Ed.), *Critical multiculturalism: Rethinking multicultural and antiracist education* (pp. 191-215). Philadelphia: Routledge Farmer.

Nieto, Sonia. (2004). *Affirming diversity: The sociopolitical context of multicultural education*. New York: Addison Wesley Longman.

Paige, R. Michael, Helen L. Jorstad, Laura Paulson, Francine Klein, & Jeanette Colby. (1999). Culture learning in language education: A review of the literature. In R. Michael Paige, Dale L. Lange & Yelena A. Yershova. (Eds.), *Culture as the core: Integrating culture into the language curriculum* (pp. 47-114). Minneapolis: Center for Advanced Research in Language Acquisition, University of Minnesota.

Palencia, Enrique Sanchez. (1998). *Meet James Gurney: Dinosaur stamp artist*. Retrieved April 2, 2002, from http://www.education-world.com/a_lesson/lesson006.shtml

Parekh, Bhikhu C. (2000). *Rethinking multiculturalism: Cultural diversity and political theory*. Cambridge, MA: Harvard University Press.

Park, Robert E. (1928). Human migration and the marginal man. *American journal of Sociology, 33*, 881-893.

Peng, Keriping, & Richard E. Nisbett. (1999). Culture, dialectics, and reasoning about contradiction. *American Psychologist, 54*, 741-754.

Perkins, D. N., & Salomon, G. (1992). Transfer of learning [Electronic Version]. *International Encyclopedia of Education* (2nd ed.). Retrieved July 7, 2007, from http://learnweb.harvard.edu/alps/thinking/docs/traencyn.htm

Perkins, David N., & Chris Unger. (1999). Teaching and learning for understanding. In Charles M. Reigeluth (Ed.), *Instructional design theories and models: A new paradigm of instructional theory* (Vol. 2, pp. 91-114). Mahwah, NJ: Erlbaum.

Piaget, Jean. (1977). *The grasp of consciousness: Action and concept in the young child*. London: Routledge & Kegan Paul.

Piaget, Jean, & Barbel Inhelder. (1967). *The child's conception of space*. New York: W. W. Norton.

Polanyi, Michael. (1967). *The tacit dimension*. London: Routledge & Kegan Paul.

Reason, Peter, & John Rowan. (Eds.). (1981). *Human inquiry: A sourcebook of new paradigm research*. New York: Wiley.

Reddy, Michael J. (1979). The Conduit Metaphor: A case of frame conflict in our language about language. In Andrew Ortony (Ed.), *Metaphor and thought* (pp. 164-201). Cambridge, England: Cambridge University Press.

Riegel, Klaus F. (1973). Dialectical operations: The final period of cognitive development. *Human Development, 18*, 430-443.

Rimmington, Glyn M., Kay Gibson, & Mara Alagic. (2007). Improving strategies for intercultural communication through simulated experiences. In Thomas Schmalzer, Gerhard Apfelthaler, Katrin Hansen & Rahul Singh (Eds.), *Intercultural communication competence: Implications for learning and teaching in a globalized world* (pp. 180-196). Delhi: Macmillan.

Rimmington, Glyn M. (2003). An introduction to global learning. *Proceedings of the 14th International Conference of the Society for Information Technology & Teacher Education (SITE 2003), Albuquerque, NM*, 1536-1539.

Rimmington, Glyn M., & Sharon Bever-Goodvin (2005). Global learning for developing intra- and inter-personal intelligences. *Proceedings of the 16th International Conference of the Society for Information Technology in Teacher Education, (SITE 2005), Phoenix, AZ,* 1750-1758.

Rimmington, Glyn M., & Kay L. Gibson. (2004). Global learning for gifted education teachers of diverse cultural backgrounds. *Proceedings of the 20th Annual Conference on Distance Teaching & Learning, Madison, Wisconsin.*

Rimmington, Glyn M., Kay L. Gibson, Ian Wesley Gibson, & Mara Alagic (2004). A cage model of global learning. *Proceedings of the 15th International Conference of the Society for Information Technology & Teacher Education International Conference (SITE 2004), Atlanta, GA, 3027-3032.*

Rimmington, Glyn M., Paul Gruba, Deborah Gordon, Kay L. Gibson, & Ian Wesley. (2004). Achieving alternative perspectives through global learning. In D. Murphy, R. Carr, J. Taylor & T. M. Wong (Eds.), *Distance education and technology: Issues and practice* (pp. 89-110). Hong Kong: Open University of Hong Kong Press.

Rimmington, Glyn M., Meg O'Reilly, Kay L. Gibson, & Deborah Gordon. (2003). Assessment strategies for global learning: I Theory. *Proceedings of the World conference on educational multimedia, hypermedia & telecommunications. Association for the Advancement of Computing in Education, (Ed-Media 2003), Honolulu, HI, 2487-2490.*

Rodgers, Carol. (2002). Defining reflection: Another look at John Dewey and reflective thinking. *Teachers College Record, 104*(4), 842-866.

Rogers, Everett M. (1999). Georg Simmel's concept of the stranger and intercultural communication research. *Communication Theory, 9*(1), 58-74.

Rosendorfer, Herbert. (1997). *Letters back to ancient China.* Sawtry, England: Dedalu.

Ruben, Brent D., & Daniel J Kealey. (1979). Behavioral assessment of communication competency and the prediction of cross-cultural adaptation. *International journal of intercultural relations, 3,* 15-47.

Rutherford, Jonathan. (Ed.). (1990). *Identity, community, culture, difference.* London: Lawrence & Wishart.

Schmid, Christian. (1999). A remote laboratory using virtual reality on the Web. *Simulation, 73*(1), 13-21.

Schoenfeld, Alan H. (1992). Learning to think mathematically: Problem solving, metacognition, and sense making in mathematics. In Douglas A. Grouws (Ed.), *Handbook of research on mathematics teaching and learning* (pp. 334-370). New York: Macmillan.

Schön, Donald A. (1987). *Educating the reflective practitioner.* San Francisco: Jossey-Bass.

Schön, Donald A. (1983). *The reflective practitioner: How professionals think in action.* New York: Basic Books.

Schunk, Dale H. (2004). *Learning theories: An educational perspective* (4th ed.). Upper Saddle River, NJ: Pearson Education.

Scott, Philip H. (1979). *The jewel in the crown.* New York: Avon.

Scott, Philip H., Eduardo Fleury Mortimer, & Orlando G. Aguiar. (2006). The tension between authoritative and dialogic discourse: A fundamental characteristic of meaning making interactions in high school science lessons. *Science Education Journal, 90,* 605-631.

Selman, Mark. (1988). Schon's gate is square but is it art? In Peter P. Grimmett & Gaalen L. Erikson (Eds.). *Reflection in teacher education* (pp. 177-192). New York: Teachers College Press.

Shannon, Claude E., & Warren Weaver. (1967). *The mathematical theory of communication.* Urbana, IL: The University of Illinois Press.

Shaw, Carolyn M. (2004). Using role-play simulations in the IR classroom: An examination of exercises on peacekeeping operations and foreign policy decision making. *International Studies Perspectives, 5,* 1-22.

Shor, Ira. (2002). *Empowering education: Critical teaching for social change.* Chicago: The University of Chicago Press.

Simmel, Georg. (1921). The social significance of the "stranger." In Robert E. Park & Ernest W. Burgess (Eds.), *Introduction to the science of sociology* (pp. 322-327). Chicago: University of Chicago Press.

Simpson, Terry. (2002). Dare I oppose constructivist theory? *The Educational Forum, 66,* 347-349.

Singerman, Alan J. (Ed.). (1996). *Acquiring cross-cultural competence. Four stages for students of French.* Lincolnwood, Il: American Association of Teachers of French National Commission on Cultural Competence. National Textbook.

Smith, G. Pritchy. (1998). *Common sense about uncommon knowledge: The knowledge bases for diversity.* Washington, DC: The American Association of Colleges for Teacher Education (AACTE).

Soschinske, Kurt Albert, Glyn M. Rimmington, & Mara Alagic. (2006). Preparation of engineering senior design course: Global learning integration. *Proceedings of the 9th International Conference on Engineering Education, San Juan, PR,* 4E-18-22.

Starosta, William J., & Guo-Ming Chen. (2005). Intercultural listening: Collected reflections, collated refractions. *International and Intercultural Communication Annual, 28,* 274-285.

Storme, Julie A., & Mana Derakhshani. (2002). Defining, teaching, and evaluating cultural proficiency in the foreign language classroom. *Foreign Language Annals, 35*(6), 657-668.

Storti, Craig. (1990). *The art of crossing cultures.* Yarmouth: Intercultural Press.

Suler, John. (1999). The palace [Electronic Version]. *New Observations: Cultures of Cyberspace, 120*(10). Retrieved September 14, 2007, from http://www-usr.rider.edu/~suler/psycyber/palacestudy.html

Sun, Xiudong D. (1989). *Atlas of the People's Republic of China.* Beijing: Foreign Languages Press.

Tam, Maureen. (2000). Constructivism, instructional design, and technology: Implications for transforming distance learning [Electronic Version]. *Educational Technology & Society, 3.* Retrieved June 20, 2007, from http://www.ifets.info/journals/3_2/tam.html

Taylor, Edward W. (1994). Intercultural competency: A transformative learning process. *Adult Education Quarterly, 44*(3), 154-174.

Taylor, Edward W. (1997). Building upon the theoretical debate: A critical review of the empirical studies of Mezirow's transformative learning theory. *Adult Education Quarterly, 48*(1), 34-59.

Taylor, Edward W. (2000). Analyzing research on transformative learning theory. In Jack Mezirow, (Ed.), *Learning as transformation: Critical perspectives on a theory in progress* (pp. 285-328). San Francisco: Jossey-Bass.

Tuleja, Elizabeth A. (2005). Intercultural communication for business. In James S. O'Rourke (Ed.), *Managerial Communication Series No 6*. Mason, OH: Thomson South-Western.

Ting-Toomey, Stella. (1999). *Communicating across cultures*. New York-London: The Guilford Press.

Ting-Toomey, Stella. (2005). The matrix of face: An updated face-negotiation theory. In William B. Gudykunst (Ed.), *Theorizing about intercultural communication* (pp. 71-93). Thousand Oaks, CA: SAGE.

Ting-Toomey, Stella, & Leeva C. Chung. (2005). *Understanding intercultural communication*. Los Angeles: Roxbury.

Tudge, Jonathan R. H., & Paul A. Winterhoff. (1993). Vygotsky, Piaget, and Bandura: Perspectives on the relations between the social world and cognitive development. *Human Development, 36*, 61-81.

United Nations Educational, Scientific and Cultural Organization. (2001). *UNESCO Universal declaration on cultural diversity*. Paper presented at the 31st Session of the General Conference of UNESCO. Retrieved June 15, 2007, from http://unesdoc.unesco.org/images/0012/001271/127160m.pdf

Vaara, Eero, Jaane Tienari, & Risto Säntti. (2003). The international match: Metaphors as vehicles of social identity-building in cross-border mergers. *Human Relations, 56*(4), 419-451.

Voloshinov, Valentin Nikolaevich. (1929/1973). *Marxism and the philosophy of language* (Ladislav Matejka & Irwin Robert Titunik, Trans.) New York: Seminar Press. (Original work published 1929)

Vygotsky, Lev Semenovich. (1978). *Mind in society: The development of higher psychological processes*. Cambridge, MA: Harvard University Press.

Vygotsky, Lev Semenovich. (1981). The genesis of higher mental functions. In James V. Wertsch (Ed.), *The concept of activity in Soviet psychology* (pp. 144-188). Armonk, NY: M. E. Sharpe.

Wang, Chun-Min, & Thomas Charles Reeves. (2007). The meaning of culture in online education: Implications for teaching, learning, and design. In Andrea Edmundson (Ed.), *Globalized e-learning cultural challenges* (pp. 1-17). Hershey, PA: Information Science.

Whitman, Lawrence E., Don E. Malzahn, Barbara S. Chaparro, Mark Russell, Rebecca Langrall, & Beth A. Mohler. (2005). A comparison of group processes, performance, and satisfaction in face-to-face versus computer-mediated engineering student design teams, *Journal of Engineering Education, 94*(3), 327-334.

Wiemann, John M., & Philip Backlund. (1980). Current theory and research in communicative competence. *Review of Educational Research, 50*, 185-199.

Wiley, David A. (Ed.). (2000). *Instructional use of learning objects*. Bloomington, IN: Association of Educational Communications and Technology.

Wills, Sandra, & Albert Ip. (2002). Online role play as a complementary learning design for the first fleet database. *Proceedings of the Australian Council for Computers in Education Conference, Hobart, Tasmania* [Online]. Retrieved August 2007, from http://www.pa.ash.org.au/acec2002/confpapers/ paperdetails.asp?orgid=1&suborgid=1&ssid=111&pid=616&ppid=0&uid =&docid=166

Wink, Joan. (2005). *Critical pedagogy: Notes from the real world* (3rd ed.). Boston: Allyn & Bacon.

Winn, William. (1993). Instructional design and situated learning: Paradox or partnership. *Educational Technology, 33(3)*, 16-21.

Witherspoon, Tonya Lynn, Karen V. Reynolds, Mara Alagic, & Gina M. Copas (2004). A model for an online, global, constructionist learning environment: Robotics around the world. *Proceedings of the 15th International Conference of the Society for Information Technology & Teacher Education. Association for Advancement of Computers in Education (SITE 2004). Atlanta, GA*, 3083-3088.

Wong, Wan-chi. (2006). Understanding dialectical thinking from a cultural-historical perspective. *Philosophical Psychology, 19*(2), 239-260.

Yeotis, Catherine, Mara Alagic, & Kay Gibson. (2004). How does a learning cycle promote self-directed learning? *Proceedings of the 6th International Conference on Education, Athens, Greece.*

Yildirim, Mehmet B., Mehmet Barut, & Kemal Kilic. (2004). A global learning experience in supply chain logistics management. *Proceedings of the 5th International Conference on Information Technology Based Higher Education and Training: ITHET '04, Istanbul, Turkey.*

Young, Iris Marion. (1990). *Justice and the politics of difference.* Princeton, NJ: Princeton University Press.

Young, Robert. (1996). *Intercultural communication: Pragmatics, genealogy, deconstruction* Philadelphia: Multilingual Matters.

ABOUT THE CONTRIBUTORS

ABOUT THE AUTHORS

Dr. Alagic is an associate professor of mathematics education at the Wichita State University. Her interest in developing intercultural communication and global learning competence has arisen from having taught internationally and in culturally diverse environments. Dr. Alagic has led efforts to incorporate cage painting simulations and scenario authoring into graduate classes at Wichita State University. She has a given invited and keynote presentations on these topics at international conferences. Dr. Alagic has published extensively in this area as well as in mathematics and mathematics education. As coleader of an early global learning project on mathematics and science education, she was a recipient of the Global Learning Course Redevelopment Team Excellence Award in 2002. In addition to integrating global learning into her own classes, she mentors other faculty and K-12 teachers to infuse cage painting and global learning into the curriculum. Her research activities have attracted numerous external grants. She received the College of Education Research Award in 2004-2005. Dr. Alagic received her PhD in mathematics from the University of Belgrade. She was a faculty member in the Mathematics Departments at the University of Belgrade, University of Sarajevo and Wichita State University and at the University of Vermont as a visiting faculty member.

Dr. Glyn Rimmington joined Wichita State University as the inaugural Boeing Distinguished Professor of global learning in 2001. He leads the

155

global learning program, (gl.wichita.edu), which is aimed at infusing intercultural communication and global learning experiences into the curriculum. His goal is to prepare graduates for life in a highly diverse, interconnected and interdependent world. In 2007, Dr. Rimmington received the Howard and Jeanne Johnston Award for Global Citizenship from the Global Learning Center of Wichita. He has over 100 refereed publications and has given many international conference keynotes. His research work has attracted over $3m in grants. Prior to that he was on faculty at the University of Melbourne first in Engineering, then in Land & Food Resources. In 1995 he set up the Multimedia Education Unit as a faculty member of the Centre for the Study of Higher Education. During the 17 years at the University of Melbourne, he participated in several collaborative projects with colleagues in the United States, the United Kingdom, Canada, Mexico, China, Japan, Thailand, and the Philippines. Since 1993, part of his research activity has involved close collaboration with colleagues in the Chinese Academy of Science and universities in several provinces. Dr. Rimmington earned his PhD from the University of Queensland, where he worked as a researcher for 5 years. He is a native of Queensland, Australia.

ABOUT THE SERIES EDITORS

Lisa A. Holtan serves as the editorial assistant in the publication of this book series *Teaching* <~> *Learning Indigenous, Intercultural Worldviews: International Perspectives on Social Justice and Human Rights*. She came to the position after a year of working as a technical assistant to the editor of the scholarly publication of the World Council for Curriculum and Instruction. Lisa has served as a peer-reviewer for several scholarly manuscripts. She presented a paper based on her completed thesis, *The Experiences of Students with Disabilities at a United States Higher Education Institution* at the St. Cloud State University Student Research Colloquium. Lisa graduated from St. Cloud State University in St. Cloud, Minnesota after a earning a master of science degree in social responsibility. She earned a bachelor of arts in criminal justice studies with a minor in human relations and multicultural relations.

Tonya Huber-Warring, PhD, founding editor of this book series, *Teaching* <~> *Learning Indigenous, Intercultural Worldviews: International Perspectives on Social Justice and Human Rights, is* passionate about meaningful inquiry that informs the challenge of global human rights. Huber was founding editor of the *Journal of Critical Inquiry into Curriculum and Instruction* (1998-2004, Caddo Gap Press, San Francisco), an international, scholarly refereed journal committed to publishing the research of graduate students focused on representing meaningful ways to exploring multicultural education and critical pedagogy in teaching <~> learning dynamics, particularly through narrative inquiry and arts-based educational research. She has also worked as an associate literary editor for *Multicultural Education* since the first issue of 1993.

As one of the 13 founding members of the National Association for Multicultural Education in 1990, Huber worked diligently to build the organization. She served more than a decade on the executive board of officers and the board of directors, chartering the first state chapter (Kansas, 1995), hosting the first national leadership institute (New Mexico, 1996) and chartering the first university chapter (Wichita State University, Kansas, 2003).

She served on the International Overseas Program Faculty, College of New Jersey, Trenton (1997 to 2005), teaching courses required for the master of education for teachers working in American international schools around the world. Her teaching and research focus on culturally responsible pedagogy, education for world citizens, Huber has presented, consulted, taught, and/or researched in more than half of the 50 states in the United States, and in England, Cyprus, Vietnam, Canada, Spain, Venezuela, Côte d'Ivoire, West Africa, South Africa, China, Australia, and Kuwait. She is the author of *Quality Learning Experiences (QLEs) for all Students* (2002), *Teaching in the Diverse Classroom* (1993), and more than 140 articles and chapters.

Huber-Warring teaches research courses for the critical pedagogy doctoral program and the master of arts in curriculum and instruction at the University of St. Thomas, Minneapolis, Minnesota. Committed to culturally responsible pedagogy she serves as the education coordinator of the social responsibility Master of Science, St. Cloud State University, St. Cloud, Minnesota, where she teaches courses in human relations and antiracist research.

ABOUT THE REVIEWERS

The editorial policy of *Teaching <~> Learning Indigenous, Intercultural Worldviews International Perspectives on Social Justice and Human Rights* provides for a series editor (serving as the lead editor) to work closely with the author(s) for each chapter accepted for publication. In issues featuring an invited guest editor, the guest editor assists in this role. The editor, editorial assistant and three to five external reviewers review each manuscript that is published as a chapter in each volume of this series. The editorial assistant provides both technical and editorial inputs required for each chapter. This volume is unique to the series in that it was submitted as a book manuscript written by two authors. The editor, editorial assistant and six external reviewers have reviewed this manuscript. The editors extend sincere appreciation to the following professionals for their critical feedback on the authors' manuscript. Ultimately, the final decisions are the responsibility of the editor, but her work could not be accomplished without the selfless, dedicated expertise of the reviewers.

Danielle Celermajer, PhD, Director of Global Studies, University of Sydney, Sydney, NSW, Australia.

Michael L. Higgins, PhD, Professor, Foreign Language Center, Yamaguchi, Japan.

Stephen Hornstein, PhD, Professor, Teacher Development, College of Education, St. Cloud State University, St. Cloud, Minnesota, USA.

Songül Kilimci, PhD, Department of Linguistics and Philology, Turkic languages, Uppsala University, Uppsala, Sweden.

Ilghiz Sinagatullin, PhD, Professor of Education, Birsk State Pedagogical Institute, Birsk, Bashkortostan, Russia.

Douglas F. Warring, PhD, Professor and Chair of Teacher Education and Director of Continuing Education, University of St. Thomas, Minneapolis, Minnesota, USA.

INDEX